GROWING UP IN CHRIST

for Serious Disciples

GROWING UP IN CHRIST

for Serious Disciples

Edited by
NEIL B. WISEMAN

NAZARENE PUBLISHING HOUSE
Kansas City, Missouri

Permission to quote from the following copyrighted versions of the Bible is acknowledged with appreciation:

The Bible: An American Translation (Goodspeed), J. M. Powis Smith, Edgar J. Goodspeed. Copyright 1923, 1927, 1948, by The University of Chicago Press.

The Bible: A New Translation (Moffatt), copyright 1954 by James A. R. Moffatt. By permission of Harper and Row, Publishers, Inc.

New American Standard Bible (NASB), © The Lockman Foundation, 1960, 1962, 1963, 1968, 1971, 1972, 1973, 1975, 1977.

New English Bible (NEB), © The Delegates of the Oxford University Press and The Syndics of the Cambridge University Press, 1961, 1970.

The Holy Bible, New International Version (NIV), copyright © 1973, 1978, 1984 by the International Bible Society.

The *Revised Standard Version of the Bible* (RSV), copyrighted 1946, 1952, © 1971, 1973.

Weymouth's New Testament in Modern English (Weymouth), by Richard Francis Weymouth. By special arrangements with James Clarke and Co., Ltd. By permission of Harper and Row, Publishers, Inc.

Contents

Introduction

Good ideas often appear quite suddenly. Good ideas that are effective and produce a desired result are rare. When a good idea appears, those who look for such things are anxious to grab hold of it and make it their own. Unfortunately, most good ideas require the application of energy for effectiveness, so those who see a new idea as a short-cut to easy success soon drop the idea in search of a better and easier one. Therefore, ideas that may have high potential for generating effectiveness lose popularity, and we call them "fads."

A few years ago, "discipleship" was seen as the newest idea for developing mature Christians. Materials were quickly produced by people from many sources, and those who saw this as an effective and *easy* method grabbed the idea with enthusiasm. Since that time, however, many of those who rushed to join the "good idea" seekers have found discipling new Christians to be energy-consuming and have drifted to a search for something easier.

There has just never been an easy way to make mature Christians. Nurture, training, and support are all very energy-consuming. As with children, who must be trained if they are to function as members of society, "babes in Christ" need and want to function appropriately in the Body of Christ. Additionally, every newborn child of God has an inner compulsion to become all that God wants. Without concentrated attention and training, the discipleship process can stretch on for an unnecessary length of time. Meanwhile, the new convert gathers information about Christian living from multiple sources. Eager and hungry, the convert hears conflicting instruction, sees contradictory models, and may become confused or frustrated.

These materials are designed to satisfy the needs of those who are "called to be saints." They are well-organized and easy to follow. Perhaps nothing one can do for a new Christian will be more welcome than that of introducing these materials and assisting in their use. Although I have seen many books, notebooks, and training manuals for discipleship, nothing I have seen is more practical and appropriate for use in the Church of the Nazarene than this.

—M. V. SCUTT
Director, Evangelism Ministries

Preface

Welcome to Discipleship

Vital contemporary Christianity recognizes two needs for discipling: (1) new converts need to understand their faith, and (2) more seasoned believers need to deepen their commitments to Christ. For this to happen in the lives of our people means that the scriptural and creedal teachings are understandable and understood. To meet this worthy purpose among the Christ followers in the Church of the Nazarene is the goal of this book.

The idea for this project was born in the hearts of the general superintendents. They challenged the writing team to produce material that would be clear, concise, and built on the foundation of the Articles of Faith in the *Manual of the Church of the Nazarene.*

After the writing team, composed of the authors of the various chapters of this book, met for the first time, it was concluded that no one person could adequately write on any one of these subjects. Consequently, a unique editing technique, seldom if ever tried in publishing efforts, was developed.

Each member of the team wrote a chapter. Then the group met for a week in marathon day and night sessions to work over every line in every chapter. With a serious commitment to produce the best possible finished product, the writing team gave its attention to Scripture, creed, interpretation, concept, writing style, and project design.

After the committee had done its work, the individual manuscripts were turned over to an editor and typist. By the end of the week, this writing-editing committee had considered three generations of manuscripts.

In the months since that week of writing and editing, the whole manuscript has been read by the Board of General Superintendents and members of the Book Committee. Every writer and every reader involved in this process has had opportunity to offer evaluations. A conscientious effort has been made to include every suggested improvement.

Dr. Eugene L. Stowe, the adviser to our committee from the Board of General Superintendents, gave wise counsel and warm affirmation.

Now that the writing effort is finished, the possible impact on the Church of the Nazarene begins. The writing team joins with local, district, and general church leaders in the prayer written by Dr. Phineas F. Bresee in 1905 that the church "may be correct in doctrine, strong in faith, and rich in divine grace."

—NEIL B. WISEMAN

GROWING UP IN CHRIST

for Serious Disciples

*The old has gone,
the new has come!*

1 COR. 5:17, NIV

Your New Life in Christ

BILL M. SULLIVAN

Carl represented what most people want in life. He had a good job, a beautiful home, a lovely family, and a circle of close friends. In short, he was enjoying the good life. He was happy and wanted to keep it that way—but he couldn't.

His first shock came when his teenage boy ran away from home. The following months were filled with efforts at reconciliation with his son. He was eager to make amends for his shortcomings as a father. He counted no cost too great to restore his son to a sensible life-style.

For the first time in his life he really needed the church, and he reached out to it. It was beautiful to see Carl getting involved in the activity and life of the congregation. The people received his whole family warmly. Everyone joined together to help them find their way into the fellowship and restore the unity of their home. They became so involved that the church assumed they had already come to know Christ personally. But that was not the case.

It was an exciting moment when they walked down the aisle and knelt at the altar. As a family, and individually, they found Jesus Christ as Savior and Lord.

BILL SULLIVAN is director of Church Growth Division at Nazarene Headquarters; formerly superintendent of North Carolina District.

When they rose from the place of prayer, it was obvious that something special had happened in their lives. They had been deeply involved in the church for several months but this experience marked the beginning of a new dimension in their love and service. They had entered into a spiritual reality. They had discovered new life in Christ.

The months and years that followed proved how great a transformation had taken place in Carl's life. What he had experienced was more than a moment of inspiration. It was a complete turnaround in his life, and the change had endured not only the wear of the years but also the hard blows of heartbreak.

ONE EVENT—MANY DESCRIPTIONS

New Birth

Carl's discovery of new life in Christ was what Jesus described to Nicodemus as being born again. "Flesh gives birth to flesh," He explained, "but the Spirit gives birth to spirit" (John 3:6, NIV). These words of Jesus describe the transformation that is produced when a man believes in Christ (v. 15).

This figure is only one of several New Testament descriptions of finding Christ. The Bible also speaks of sonship by adoption (Gal. 4:4-7) and being found when one is lost (Luke 15:10).

New Creation

Paul says becoming a Christian is like being created again. "Therefore, if anyone is in Christ, he is a new creation; the old has gone, the new has come!" (2 Cor. 5:17, NIV). This is more than a new beginning; it is a new nature. We usually refer to this as being converted. That part of the nature that is commonly called character is truly transformed. "The old has gone, the new has come!"

The transformation of Saul of Tarsus (Paul) is a perfect illustration of one who becomes a new creature in Christ. He traveled from Jerusalem to Damascus, planning to take Christians as prisoners. "Suddenly a light from heaven flashed around him. He fell to the ground and heard a voice say to him, 'Saul, Saul, why do you persecute me?' 'Who are you, Lord?' Saul asked. 'I am Jesus, whom you are persecuting,' he replied. 'Now get up and go into the city, and you will be told what you must do'" (Acts 9:3-6, NIV).

From that moment, Saul ceased his bitter persecution of the Christians and became a devout servant of Jesus Christ. His conversion was spectacular, but it reflects the radical transformation of character when an avowed enemy of Christ is converted. A similar dramatic change is seen when Zacchaeus encountered Jesus. He offered to repay fourfold any money he had gained illegally. The demon-possessed maniac of Gadara became a transformed man, "dressed and in his right mind" (Mark 5:15, NIV; cf. vv. 1-20). You will also be moved by the transformation of a young woman, the Philippian fortune-teller (Acts 16:16-18); and the conversion of the Philippian jailer (vv. 22-34).

Restoration

But transformation of attitude and life-style is only one part of Christian conversion. Jesus declared that He came "to seek and to save what was lost" (Luke 19:10, NIV). People are separated from God as a result of sin—disobedience to His law and unfair treatment of other persons. This estrangement means that their lives are out of step with God's purpose; they are missing much that God has planned for them. Christian conversion is restoration and recovery. In Christ one is restored to fellowship with God. In that restored fellowship he recovers fullness of life known only to those who walk with God.

Deliverance

Rescue is another aspect of Christian conversion. Sin brings a consciousness of guilt that is sometimes intolerable. To be the object of God's wrath (Eph. 2:1-3), and to have the sentence of spiritual death pronounced upon us, is a fearsome thing. When guilty and condemned it is good news to learn that "Christ died for the ungodly" (Rom. 5:6). Christian conversion saves us from the consequences of sin that make life unhappy here. And to be converted is to be rescued from the penalty of separation from God throughout eternity.

Eternal Life

The idea of spiritual death is contrasted with the gift of eternal life. Whoever believes in Christ "shall not perish but have eternal life" (John 3:16, NIV). Jesus explains that His gift is more than endless life. Rather, it is a quality of life, a relationship to God both here and hereafter. "Now this is eternal life: that they may know you, the only true God, and Jesus Christ, whom you have sent" (John 17:3, NIV). This was the new life in Christ that Carl and his family found as they sought for God at the altar of prayer.

REFLECTING ON OUR EXPERIENCE

The Scriptures do not attempt a systematic arrangement of the concepts of Christian conversion. But the church has tried to arrange the various ideas in a natural sequence that reflects the biblical truths.

The Articles of Faith in the Church of the Nazarene are the official statements of our understanding of what the Bible teaches about God and His will for man. The teachings on Christian conversion are covered in three main headings: Article VII. Free Agency, Article VIII. Repentance, and Article IX. Justification, Regeneration, and Adoption. In these articles we find seven facets, but all are parts of the shining truth of Christian conversion.

VII. *Free Agency*

... the grace of God through Jesus Christ is freely bestowed upon all men, enabling all who will to turn from sin to righteousness, believe on Jesus Christ for pardon and cleansing from sin, and follow good works pleasing and acceptable in His sight.

The Grace of God

The grace of God refers to His gifts to us. We do not deserve any of them. That is why we sometimes define grace as *unmerited favor*. God's free gifts show His love and mercy. Prevenient grace includes all of God's blessings that come to us before we come to Christ. The Bible says, "God demonstrates his own love for us in this: While we were still sinners, Christ died for us" (Rom. 5:8, NIV). This grace is important because before we find the new life we are "dead in trespasses and sins." Such a person has no power to come to Christ.

When the Holy Spirit, through conscience, begins to prod and conviction grips our emotions, this is part of God's inviting and enabling grace that comes before salvation.

This prevenient grace shows that a person is not saved by "works," that is, by some self-generated action. Salvation, from beginning to end, is by grace. The Bible clearly declares, "For it is by grace you have been saved, through faith—and this not from yourselves, it is the gift of God—not by works, so that no one can boast" (Eph. 2:8-9, NIV).

VIII. *Repentance*

We believe that repentance, which is a sincere and thorough change of the mind in regard to sin, involving a sense of personal guilt and a voluntary turning away from sin, is demanded of all who have by act or purpose become sinners against God. . . .

Repentance

To repent is to admit our guilt for sins and to declare a sincere intention to make things right.

The sense of guilt is created when the Holy Spirit shows us how we have broken God's law. This is the divine initiative in repentance. A person never repents without a sense of conviction of guilt for sins—and he is never seized by such an awareness without the gracious aid of the Spirit of God.

God's initiative must be followed by our response. Repentance is incomplete until conviction for sin is followed by a change in direction on our part. Repentance is a complete change of mind about sin, a contrite sorrow for the sins we have committed, and a turning away from sin.

The forsaking of sin is the human part of repentance. It is a person's response to the call of God and to the drawing influence of the Spirit. Without the action of the will to turn from sin to God, there is no true repentance and consequently no conversion to the new life in Christ.

But even in our response to God's call we do not act in our own strength. God is at work in us, as the *Manual* states:

The Spirit of God gives to all who will repent the gracious help of penitence of heart and hope of mercy, that they may believe unto pardon and spiritual life.

Faith

Faith for salvation is trusting Jesus Christ for spiritual restoration and transformation. It is based on what the *Manual* calls "hope of mercy, that they may believe unto pardon and spiritual life."

We believe God's promise to give new life to all who repent. Thus faith and repentance go together; they are two sides of the same coin. "Repent and believe the good news!" (Mark 1:15, NIV). They comprise the human response to God's call. As repentance is turning from sin, faith is turning to Christ.

Faith, like repentance, is made possible by God. He gives the power to believe. Without faith no person can place his trust in Christ. But God does not believe for us. He graciously gives the power to believe, but that is not the same thing as the act of believing. We must choose to place our trust in Christ. When that decision is made, the person receives the experience of Christian conversion that brings new life in Christ.

IX. *Justification, Regeneration, and Adoption*

We believe that justification is the gracious and judicial act of God by which He grants full pardon of all guilt and complete release from the penalty of sins committed, and acceptance as righteous, to all who believe on Jesus Christ and receive Him as Lord and Savior. . . .

Justification

The change that Carl experienced at the altar is described in three ways. The first is God's work of justification. Justification "is God's full pardon; He takes away our guilt and cancels the penalty of the sins we have committed." Paul declares, "I want you to know that through Jesus the forgiveness of sins is proclaimed to you. Through him everyone who believes is justified from everything you could not be justified from by the law of Moses" (Acts 13:38-39, NIV).

God justifies us because of the work of Jesus Christ. As Paul explains, "He was delivered over to death for our sins and was raised to life for our justification" (Rom. 4:25, NIV).

> We believe that regeneration, or the new birth, is that gracious work of God whereby the moral nature of the repentant believer is spiritually quickened and given a distinctively spiritual life, capable of faith, love, and obedience. . . .

Regeneration

God's work of regeneration is the renewing aspect of Christian conversion. It means "to be again." This describes spiritual renewal of human life. It involves changes that the Bible variously calls "born again," "born of God," "born of the Spirit," "quickened," and "passed from death unto life."

This new life in Christ is entirely the work of God in the spirit of a person. In repentance and faith, the person is capable of response and required to respond through the enabling of the Holy Spirit. But regeneration is exclusively God's act in us. The Holy Spirit breathes new life into the soul that before was "dead in your transgressions and sins" (Eph. 2:1, NIV). With this new spirit we find a new faith in God; we discover a deep love for Him and a great desire to obey what He tells us to do.

To be regenerated is to begin the experience of being made like God in our desires and decisions. To be like God is to be holy. Thus we sometimes speak of regeneration as initial holiness—God's first action in making us like himself.

> We believe that adoption is that gracious act of God by which the justified and regenerated believer is constituted a son of God. . . .

Adoption   Gal 4:4-7

Paul uses this term to show that when we have been converted we become members of God's family with all the family privileges. He writes, "You did not receive a spirit that makes you a slave again to fear, but you received the Spirit of sonship [adoption]. And by him we cry, '*Abba*, Father.' The Spirit himself testifies with our spirit that we are God's children. Now if we are children, then we are heirs—heirs of God and co-heirs with Christ" (Rom. 8:15-17, NIV).

> We believe that justification, regeneration, and adoption are simultaneous in the experience of seekers after God and are obtained upon the condition of faith, preceded by repen-

tance; and that to this work and state of grace the Holy Spirit
bears witness.

The Witness of the Spirit

Justification, regeneration, and adoption all occur at the same
time when we are converted. The Bible uses this language to describe to us what God does for us when we repent and believe for
salvation. Although we cannot separate these elements in our experience, we know that a great transformation has taken place.
This knowledge we call the witness of the Spirit.

This witness of the Holy Spirit is the assurance that God
communicates to us. It is the inward evidence that God gives us
so that we can be sure of His love and acceptance. The Scriptures
declare, "The Spirit himself testifies with our spirit that we are
God's children" (Rom. 8:16, NIV). And again, "Because you are
sons, God sent the Spirit of his Son into our hearts, the Spirit who
calls out, '*Abba*, Father'" (Gal. 4:6, NIV). John tells us, "Anyone
who believes in the Son of God has this testimony in his heart" (1
John 5:10, NIV).

This witness of the Spirit is direct. It is more than a logical
inference that something has happened to us. It cannot be fully
explained but is readily recognizable in the heart of a believer. It is
God's Spirit impressing our spirit with the reality that we are children of God.

Again—One Event with Many Descriptions

At this point it is important to remember that all these aspects of conversion take place at the point of faith. God is always
extending the *grace* that prepares and enables a sinner to respond
to Him. Then when the sinner comes to a point of *repentance*,
faith for salvation is usually not far behind. When *faith* is exer-
cised, God *justifies*, *regenerates*, and *adopts* us in the same moment. Usually the *witness of the Spirit* is realized at the same time
although in some instances it may come later.

Justification and assurance are not the same. God freely for-
gives us when we repent and believe. But He then graciously assures us that we belong to Him.

I Must Be Born Again

Now that we have considered what new life in Christ means, Christ confronts us with the question: Have I experienced the new birth in my life? This wonderful experience is available to all; it is also required of all who seek a right relationship with God and who hope to find everlasting life.

It Is for Me

Carl had found fellowship in the church, but he had not yet found Christ. The day came when God spoke to him with conviction. The Bible declares, "Now is the time of God's favor, now is the day of salvation" (2 Cor. 6:2, NIV). If we have not found Him, there is no better time to find Christ than at this very moment. Would you respond to the call of God's Spirit in your life? Would you like to be born again? Would you pray?

O God, I realize that I am a sinner. I have broken Your law and rebelled against Your will. I have insisted on living life my own way. I am sorry for my sins and confess them to You right now. I not only acknowledge my sins but I turn my back on them. I do not want to live in opposition to Your will any longer. Please forgive me and help me to live for You.

I believe that You died to take away the sins of the whole world. I believe that You died to forgive *my* sins.

Just now as I confess my sins, I look up to You in faith, believing that You forgive my sins and save me from them.

Thank You, Lord, it is true. You do forgive sins. I believe it with all my heart. I praise You for saving me from my sins and for giving me new life in Christ.

O Father, how I thank You that You have made me one of Your own children. I praise You for receiving me into the family of God. AMEN.

Thank You, Lord

With the assurance of salvation comes a deep sense of gratitude to God. The conviction of guilt for sin is gone. In its place there is peace. But there is an even greater reason for gratitude.

New life in Christ was made possible by our Lord at a tremendous cost. He died on the Cross for our sins. His sacrificial act revealed both the tragedy of sin and the eternal worth of a person. The price He paid shows how important our salvation is to Him. He knows that human beings can be restored to all that God has planned for them.

Conversion brings a deep sense of gratitude. Our self-worth is affirmed. We know that we belong to God's family. Our human personality experiences its greatest sense of meaning in this climate of God's acceptance and fellowship.

The Affirmation of Baptism

The Scriptures are very clear that Christians should declare the reality of their conversion by being baptized. In line with this, Article of Faith XII reads as follows:

> We believe that Christian baptism, commanded by our Lord, is a sacrament signifying acceptance of the benefits of the atonement of Jesus Christ, to be administered to believers and declarative of their faith in Jesus Christ as their Savior, and full purpose of obedience in holiness and righteousness. . . .
>
> Baptism may be administered by sprinkling, pouring, or immersion, according to the choice of the applicant (*Manual*, par. 16).

We are not saved by this or any other ordinance, but by submitting to baptism we are saying to God and to others, "I have given my life to God, I have received Christ as my Savior, and I mean to follow Him all my days."

We believe that being baptized is honoring God and follows the example of Jesus himself who, as He began His ministry, was baptized by John in the Jordan River (Matt. 3:13; Mark 1:9; Luke 3:21). We believe also that it follows the example of the Early Church, for we read in Acts 2:41, "Those who accepted his message were baptized" (NIV).

Tell the Good News

That a person can experience new life in Christ is good news. Most of the world has never heard that message. Most of the people who have heard it learned about Christ from someone who had already met Him. The most convincing witness of the Good News is the radiant life and personal testimony of a person who has been born again.

When we have experienced new life in Christ, we want to share our faith with our family and friends. It is really too good to keep.

His Church and Yours

Part of belonging to God's family is belonging to Christ's Church. Jesus declared, "I will build my church" (Matt. 16:18). It is His Church. All who have been born again are members of it. The Bible states, "The Lord added to their number daily those who were being saved" (Acts 2:47, NIV).

The Church of Jesus Christ is worldwide; it includes all who have trusted in Christ for salvation. But the Church is made up of local congregations. Every believer should find a place in some Christian fellowship where God is worshiped and the Good News is preached.

ONLY A BEGINNING

New life in Christ is wonderful. But it is only the beginning. It is not the goal, but the gate. Conversion is to be followed by living out the new life, and learning how to serve Christ better. *Disciple* is the term used to describe a follower of Jesus Christ. A disciple is one who seeks to learn about and practice the teachings of his Master.

Just as physical birth is the beginning of a human life that continues to grow and develop to maturity, so the new birth is the starting point for spiritual growth and development. Stretching out before us is a life of challenging proportions. As Jesus expressed it, "If anyone would come after me, he must deny himself and take up his cross daily and follow me. For whoever wants to save his life will lose it, but whoever loses his life for me will save it" (Luke 9:23-24, NIV).

Thank You, Lord, for calling me. Thank You for saving me. Thank You for letting me walk through life by Your side.

For our sake he made him to be sin who knew no sin, so that in him we might become the righteousness of God.

2 COR. 5:21, RSV

Who Provided This New Life?

AL TRUESDALE

Brad edged his way into the office coffee room and sat down beside his friend Kent. He had often chatted with Kent over such wide-ranging topics as vacation spots, real estate, sports, investments, and professional advancement.

Occasionally the conversation touched on religion, but that had not been of particular interest to Brad. Nor was Kent strongly inclined toward spiritual matters. Brad was known as a church member and he lived a clean life, but that was about as far as it went.

But three weeks ago, Brad experienced a turnaround in his life; he had become a born-again Christian. A new interest now completely dominated his thinking. Kent was a little bewildered. What had come over his friend?

Brad had a deepening realization of what knowing Christ as one's personal Savior really meant. A new perspective was shaping his life. God who such a short time before had been ignored was now at the center of his thoughts. Kent could not quite comprehend what had happened but there was no denying the transformation. For Brad it was the beginning of an exciting pilgrimage, a new adventurous life in Christ.

AL TRUESDALE is academic dean and professor of philosophy and Christian ethics at Nazarene Theological Seminary, Kansas City.

The new birth does, indeed, launch the Christian into a lifetime of growth. He desires a better understanding of what God has begun and now continues to do in his life.

LIFE'S NEW DIRECTION

The profound change that Christ brings about in the life of the new Christian is not merely an emotional or psychological experience. It is the testimony of God to him that he has become one with Him. The New Testament says plainly, "By this we know that we abide in him and he in us, because he has given us of his own Spirit. . . . Whoever confesses that Jesus is the Son of God, God abides in him, and he in God" (1 John 4:13, 15, RSV). Christians are alive with a new life not of their own making. "The life [we] now live in the flesh [we] live by faith in the Son of God, who loved [us] and gave himself for [us]" (Gal. 2:20, RSV).

All of this is a joyous certainty for the Christian. So we can confidently express this reality in song, in word, and in our way of life.

But the experience of the new birth is not an end in itself. New life in Christ leads to a major redirection of life, away from the self-centeredness that characterized the old life. The "self" is no longer the main object of consideration. Paul's admonition in this matter is vital: "Those who live [in Christ should] live no longer for themselves but for him who for their sake died and was raised" (2 Cor. 5:15, RSV). This new life in Christ causes us to seek the will of God, and the good of our fellowmen.

The essence of sinning is that we turn from God and enthrone ourselves as the center of life. This self-centeredness means that the whole world, and even God himself, exists to be exploited for our own satisfaction. It cannot and will not bring glory to God (Rom. 8:7). True human fulfillment is impossible under these circumstances.

Our age is dominated by such self-centeredness. Walter Lippmann described this spirit and attitude as an "acid" that destroys society. The problem is that when a person lives for self there is no divine authority in his life. There is nothing left to check his willfulness and greed. And there is no unifying purpose through which he can find meaning for existence.

There is a danger that this self-interest will be seen as the end purpose of God's presence in us. If this happens, the horizons of God's grace collapse into the narrow dimensions of the human ego. All that God accomplished in this person's life would be compressed into one word, *"Me!"* This error may be seen in some religious music and literature where the word *I* is dominant to the exclusion of worship of God and expressed concern for others.

But our pattern is Christ; His chief purpose was to glorify the Father by doing His will (John 17:4). His selfless devotion to His Heavenly Father becomes the Christian's model of what one's relationship to God should be.

The fulfillment of the new life in Christ lies in a major reorientation of the self toward God. The result is a true worship of God and a deep desire to do His will on earth.

The fundamental reason for Christian rejoicing and hope is not that Christ is in *us* but that by grace we are in *Him.* Christians are to have steadfast faith in Christ (Col. 2:5); to walk in Christ Jesus the Lord (v. 6); to be rooted and built up in Him (v. 7); and to be made complete in Him (v. 10).

THE MEANING OF GOD'S SOVEREIGNTY

The Bible speaks of God as Lord, as Ruler, and as Master. But His sovereignty is not merely unlimited authority or power. It is not the unbridled omnipotence of a cosmic dictator who simply "does whatever he wants to." Rather, God's sovereignty is His freedom to be the God of holy love. His sovereignty is not a threat to us; it is His promise that He will be himself and true to His creation.

God's sovereignty is revealed in His creative and saving deeds, and reaches its highest expression in the coming of His Son to be the Savior of mankind. "In Christ God was reconciling the world to himself, not counting their trespasses against them . . . For our sake he made him to be sin who knew no sin, so that in him we might become the righteousness of God" (2 Cor. 5:19, 21, RSV). This sovereignty is also demonstrated in the far-reaching dimensions of His reconciliation. He was "not wishing that any should perish, but that all should reach repentance" (2 Pet. 3:9, RSV; cf. 1 Tim. 2:6; Acts 13:39, 47).

The sovereignty of God is thus a cause for Christian rejoicing. This radical recentering of life in God does not mean a loss of one's self but rather a magnificent gain. It is a restoration of one's true center in God even as it was in creation. Christ's Lordship has been reestablished in the heart and mind of the believer.

THE MEANING OF CHRIST'S COMING

That first-century, New Testament Church knew that in Jesus, the resurrected Lord, it had met the covenant-making God of Israel. They knew that in the authoritative word of deliverance spoken by Christ, the Messianic promises of God were fulfilled. And they knew that in the Spirit of the resurrected Christ, God was present with them.

The introduction to John's Gospel declares, "The Word became flesh, and dwelt among us" (NASB). We use the term *incarnation* to describe Christ's birth by which God became one with mankind in Jesus. He took upon himself not only our humanity but also our sins, even though He was without sin (2 Cor. 5:21). In Jesus of Nazareth we do not simply meet a unique messenger or the highest prophet from God. In Him we meet God himself who identifies with every level of our human existence.

The Nicene Creed of A.D. 325 is one of the most universally accepted statements of what we believe about the deity of our Lord. It affirms in part:

> We believe in one God the Father all sovereign, maker of heaven and earth, and of all things visible and invisible; and in one Lord Jesus Christ, the only begotten Son of God, begotten of the Father before all the ages, light of light, true God of true God, begotten not made, of one substance with the Father, through whom all things were made; who for us men and for our salvation came down from the heavens, and was made flesh of the Holy Spirit and the Virgin Mary and became man, and was crucified for us under Pontius Pilate, and suffered and was buried, and rose again on the third day accord-

ing to the Scriptures, and ascended into the heavens, and sitteth on the right hand of the Father, and cometh again with glory to judge living and dead, of whose kingdom there shall be no end.

The New Testament does not use the word *incarnation,* but it abounds with the meaning of the term. Col. 2:9 speaks of Christ's relationship with the "Godhead," and in Phil. 2:6-8 (RSV) we read: "Though he was in the form of God, [he] did not count equality with God a thing to be grasped, but emptied himself, taking the form of a servant, being born in the likeness of men. And being found in human form he humbled himself and became obedient unto death, even death on a cross."

Christ's saving work cuts across old religious, racial, national, and social divisions. He ended the separation of man from God and man from man. So significant was this effect that it could only be described as a new birth, a new creation, the coming of the kingdom of God, and eternal life. To sinful man this new birth was a reality comparable to the original creation. Since only the eternal God could be the Creator, could the victorious Redeemer be less? God, who spoke the world into being in creation, is the same God who meets us as Savior in Jesus. Salvation is of God; He is our Redeemer. Such is the magnitude of this new life in Christ.

The Apostles' Creed, perhaps the earliest Christian creed, declares the deity of Christ:

> I believe in God the Father Almighty, Maker of heaven and earth;
> And in Jesus Christ, His only Son, our Lord; who was conceived by the Holy Spirit, born of the Virgin Mary, suffered under Pontius Pilate, was crucified, dead, and buried; the third day He arose again from the dead; He ascended into heaven, and sitteth at the right hand of God the Father Almighty; from thence He shall come to judge the quick and the dead.
> I believe in the Holy Spirit, the holy catholic Church,* the communion of saints, the forgiveness of sins, the resurrection of the body, and the life everlasting. Amen.

The Second Article of Faith of the Church of the Nazarene is the affirmation of our belief in the deity of Christ:

---

*The Church universal.

> We believe in Jesus Christ, the Second Person of the Triune Godhead; that He was eternally one with the Father; that He became incarnate by the Holy Spirit and was born of the Virgin Mary, so that two whole and perfect natures, that is to say the Godhead and manhood, are thus united in one Person very God and very man, the God-man.
>
> We believe that Jesus Christ died for our sins, and that He truly arose from the dead and took again His body, together with all things appertaining to the perfection of man's nature, wherewith He ascended into heaven and is there engaged in intercession for us (*Manual*, par. 2).

Christianity declares not only the deity of our Lord but His full humanity as well. Since the object of God's redemption is the whole person, nothing less than the full humanity and the full deity of our Lord is adequate for fulfilling His saving purposes.

Faith in Christ, then, is faith in the Creator God who became incarnate to make possible our salvation. God's incarnation in Christ profoundly but simply means "God with us" in every dimension of life.

In the Christian sense all our knowledge about God stems from God's self-disclosure in Jesus. As one has said, "All the promises of God find their fulfillment in Christ." This self-disclosure is related to God's redeeming activity in both the Old and New Testaments.

The Christian knows who God is and what He is like through Christ's ministry, passion, death, and resurrection. He takes our sins upon himself and thereby reveals His love to us. "He hath made him to be sin for us, who knew no sin; that we might be made the righteousness of God in him" (2 Cor. 5:21).

THE NATURE OF GOD

God Is One

Judaism and Christianity are monotheistic faiths. That is, they believe that there is only one God. As sole Creator, Sustainer, and Redeemer of all, He makes any other so-called gods unnecessary. All other powers are dependent upon Him. "There is none like unto the Lord our God" (Exod. 8:10).

The supreme affirmation of the One God is central in Jewish worship. "Hear, O Israel: The Lord our God is one Lord: and thou shalt love the Lord thy God with all thine heart, and with all thy soul, and with all thy might" (Deut. 6:4-5). This is called the Shema. This is reaffirmed by Jesus in Mark 12:29-30 and becomes the Christian's affirmation as well.

God Is Holy Love

1. God is holy because of who He is and what He is. He alone is God. His nature determines the definition of holiness.

In His presence, our proper response is worship and awe. Before Him we cry, "Holy, holy, holy, Lord God Almighty" (Rev. 4:8). His glory cannot be shared. With the Old Testament writer, we exult, "Thine is the kingdom, O Lord, and thou art exalted as head above all" (1 Chron. 29:11).

To say that God is holy does not mean that He measures up to some lofty moral standard. No. He *is* holiness and what He *wills* is holy and good. The only way for the creation to be holy is to be as God wills it.

So to be true to himself, God must oppose all that is contrary to His holiness. "I am the Lord your God: ye shall therefore sanctify yourselves, and ye shall be holy; for I am holy" (Lev. 11:44). The holiness of God is ultimately revealed in the ministry and passion of Christ, and by the presence of the resurrected Lord in the Church.

2. God is love. The Bible says, "God is love; and he that dwelleth in love dwelleth in God, and God in him" (1 John 4:16). God's holiness cannot be understood apart from His love, nor can His love be understood apart from His holiness. One completes the other.

The love of God for us dominates the pages of both Old and New Testaments. "I have loved thee with an everlasting love: therefore with lovingkindness have I drawn thee" (Jer. 31:3). The ultimate expression of that love is found in Christ: "God so loved the world, that he gave his only begotten Son, that whosoever believeth in him should not perish, but have everlasting life" (John 3:16). John exclaims, "Behold, what manner of love the Father hath bestowed upon us, that we should be called the sons of God" (1 John 3:1).

God's love and His grace must be understood together. The word *grace* describes the way God deals with mankind. Grace is God's loving activity toward us despite our unworthiness.

The New Testament uses the word *agape* (a-*ga*-pay) when speaking of God's love. His love is not earned by any act or service on man's part. God steadfastly loves the unlovely. And what is more, God loves, and continues to love, even when His love is not returned.

The good news is that "God, who is rich in mercy, for his great love wherewith he loved us, even when we were dead in sins, hath quickened us together with Christ" (Eph. 2:4-5). This is the heart of the Christian gospel and its source of power.

God Reveals the Nature of Sin

Only in the light of God's love and holiness can the blight of sin be understood. That we have all "sinned and come short of the glory of God" is not a judgment leveled against us by a church, or even by ourselves, but by the One God who is holy love.

1. Sin is not primarily a matter of doing something wrong. Sin is man's refusal to obey God or submit to His will. It is man's rebellious challenge to the Almighty. When he says, "No God for me," the sinner wants God banished from his world, or relegated to insignificance, so that self may be enthroned. Even the person who prides himself on his own moral achievements is in so doing declaring his independence from God.

2. Sin is both *act* and *disposition*. The Christian faith distinguishes between acts of sin and original sin. The first sin was Adam's act of disobedience, and the sinful disposition produced by his act is known as original sin. The fall of Adam has corrupted the human race. So mankind as a whole now lives in alienation from God until he receives the redemption of Christ.

Sin is an inclination before it becomes an act. It is not merely disobedience to a law that makes an act sinful but the fact that it expresses a person's rebellion against God. Sin separates us from God.

As an individual act, sin carries with it responsibility and personal guilt. In every act of sin the universal tragedy of separation from God is confirmed and compounded.

3. All sin is expressed in one of three basic ways: as unbelief, as pride, or as self-gratification.

a. Unbelief is the act in which man turns away from God. It is separation from God in the center of one's being. Augustine said that unbelief is love turned away from God to self. This was the essence of the serpent's lie, "You will not die" (Gen. 3:4, RSV).

b. Pride is the other side of unbelief. It is making one's self the center of his world. The serpent's promise to Eve was that eating from the tree of knowledge would make her equal to God. Pride is the self-elevation of man, claiming for himself what belongs to God alone.

c. Self-gratification (called in the Scriptures "lasciviousness" or "concupiscence") includes all works of the flesh. It is the uncontrolled desire to use nature and/or other people to gratify one's own desires and pride. It reduces other people to being merely means to an end. It involves physical appetites including human sexuality, knowledge, power (including material wealth), and spiritual pride. Such sin is the sworn enemy of all true human relationships, whether domestic, social, or religious.

God Is Triune

The Christian faith affirms that the One God is essentially threefold in His being—Father, Son, and Holy Spirit. The Scriptures clearly declare the deity of the Father, the Son, and the Holy Spirit. This Christian doctrine of the Trinity is essential to Christian faith and practice.

1. The first three Articles of Faith of the Church of the Nazarene state our concept of God (*Manual,* pars. 1-3).

The First Article is titled "The Triune God":

> We believe in one eternally existent, infinite God, Sovereign of the universe; that He only is God, creative and administrative, holy in nature, attributes, and purpose; that He, as God, is Triune in essential being, revealed as Father, Son, and Holy Spirit.

The Second Article affirms the deity of Jesus Christ: "We believe in Jesus Christ, the Second Person of the Triune Godhead; that He was eternally one with the Father" (par. 2).

The Third Article testifies to our faith in the deity of the Holy Spirit:

> We believe in the Holy Spirit, the Third Person of the Triune Godhead, that He is ever present and efficiently active in and with the Church of Christ, convincing the world of sin, regenerating those who repent and believe, sanctifying believers, and guiding into all truth as it is in Jesus (par. 3).

These Articles of Faith are true to the Christian Church's historic affirmation.

Christian faith in God the Father is at the same time faith in Christ and in the Holy Spirit. The Son and the Spirit are not independent beings by the side of God the Father. None of the three can be eliminated or minimized without destroying the Christian faith at its center.

2. The doctrine of the Trinity and belief in one God. No divine act can be ascribed to one Person of the Godhead to the exclusion of the others. It is improper, for example, to ascribe the work of salvation more to the Son than to the Father. In the same manner, the work of the Holy Spirit, such as in entire sanctification, must not be separated from the work of the Father and the Son.

In our day, when the word *person* indicates a clearly distinct individual, the phrase "three Persons in one Godhead" is much more difficult for us to manage than it was for Christians of ancient times. Then the word *person* did not give the idea of independent individuality such as it does today. Because of this difference, we today must guard against understanding the doctrine of the Trinity as teaching a sort of "tritheism"—three gods.

3. The Trinity and salvation. When Christian faith speaks of God's act of salvation as the work of the Holy Spirit, it does not intend to distinguish this work from the continuing activity of Christ. The presence and activity of Christ is a presence and activity *in* the Spirit. Christ is effectively present wherever the Spirit in word and deed makes real the love of God. The New Testament affirms that Christ is life, that He gives life, and that He dwells in our hearts through faith by the Holy Spirit (Eph. 3:16-17). Life in Christ is life lived through the Spirit.

The distinct work of the Holy Spirit is to bear witness to the Lordship of Jesus Christ (John 16:5-15). He also calls, gathers, enlightens, and sanctifies. Through "the means of grace" He establishes and develops His community of saints. To know the presence of the Holy Spirit is to know the presence of the resurrected Lord. The apostle Paul underscores this oneness by repeatedly referring to the Holy Spirit as the Spirit of Christ.

Where the Spirit of God is, there God himself is. Just as the Father and the Son are personalities, so the Holy Spirit is a real person. The Holy Spirit assures us that God is not distant and that He is not an isolated being who sits enthroned far away in the heavens. He is very near. The Holy Spirit is the Spirit of love and holiness. He stands in uncompromising opposition to evil. He is the wooing, seeking, forgiving, sanctifying God among men.

*   *   *

Brad's new life in Christ was a gift from God. Now, he had an increasing eagerness to do God's will and to more fully comprehend the teachings of Scripture. He had a growing desire to learn and to let the Lord lead him into a deeper knowledge of spiritual matters.

A commitment to new truth, eagerness to live a life that is pleasing to God, and continual association with the family of God helped increase Brad's understanding of God's purposes. The same is true for every serious Christian.

*Heaven and earth
will pass away,
but my words will
never pass away.*

MATT. 24:35, NIV

God's Instructions for This New Life

NEIL B. WISEMAN

After weeks of struggle, Eric Jackson began to question his conversion. He had come to know Christ two months earlier when, during a period of special need in his own life, the personal evangelism team called at his door.

Over a period of several weeks, Eric lost his job, experienced financial difficulty, suffered through his first major illness, and felt the awful pain caused by his oldest son's divorce. Up until this time, Eric and his wife, Susan, had lived a rather trouble-free life. They had given all their efforts to achieving secular success. But Eric was devastated when his world began to crumble. He did not know where to turn for help. It seemed as though everything of importance was slipping from his grasp. Just when he was desperate for answers, the people from the church called in his home with the good news of the gospel.

Of course, Eric and Susan were interested. They wanted to know more and listened eagerly as their visitors told of what Christ could mean in their lives. That night, in response to their prayers of repentance and faith, they found Christ in their own living room.

NEIL B. WISEMAN is academic dean at Nazarene Bible College, Colorado Springs, and editor of *Grow* magazine.

The people from the church told them that the Holy Spirit had directed the evangelism team to the Jackson home that night. And all of this sounded so right.

Now two months had passed. The Jacksons' attendance at church had been consistent. The friendly acceptance of the church people encouraged them. But they were concerned because there was so much about Christianity they had not grasped. How could they learn the meaning of their faith in Christ? How could they understand the demands of Christ on their life-style? How could they know and understand the rich meaning of the promises of God that their pastor and other mature Christians so joyously discussed? And how could they be sure that the instructions they received from more experienced Christians were actually God's will for them?

This frustration brought the Jacksons, their church family, and their pastor to the conclusion that they really needed to study the Scriptures more. Here was to be found the resources for spiritual growth. Eric experienced great self-understanding when he said, "If all else fails, read the directions."

WHAT THE BIBLE SAYS ABOUT ITSELF

The Bible's testimony about itself is convincing. Here's what it says:

The Bible Will Stand Forever

The Scripture affirms, "Heaven and earth shall pass away, but my words shall not pass away" (Matt. 24:35); "All flesh is as grass, and all the glory of man as the flower of grass. The grass withereth, and the flower thereof falleth away: but the word of the Lord endureth for ever. And this is the word which by the gospel is preached unto you" (1 Pet. 1:24-25); "For ever, O Lord, thy word is settled in heaven" (Ps. 119:89).

The Bible Is Divinely Inspired

The testimony of the Word says: "All scripture is given by inspiration of God, and is profitable for doctrine, for reproof, for correction, for instruction in righteousness: that the man of God may be perfect, throughly furnished unto all good works" (2 Tim. 3:16-17); "The prophecy came not in old time by the will of man: but holy men of God spake as they were moved by the Holy Ghost" (2 Pet. 1:21).

The Bible Causes Conviction

It makes us see ourselves as we really are. "The word of God is quick, and powerful, and sharper than any twoedged sword, piercing even to the dividing asunder of soul and spirit, and of the joints and marrow, and is a discerner of the thoughts and intents of the heart" (Heb. 4:12).

The Bible Introduces Us to Christ

The Scriptures bear witness to Christ and Christ bears witness to the Scriptures. Aided by the Holy Spirit as we read, the printed words of Scripture lead us to a better understanding of Jesus. Our Lord explained this relationship to the Pharisees of His day, "You search the scriptures, because you think that in them you have eternal life; and it is they that bear witness to me; yet you refuse to come to me that you may have life" (John 5:39-40, RSV). The written Word—the Bible—points us to the Living Word —Jesus Christ. So the Scriptures do not provide salvation, rather they are used by God as an instrument to bring us to Christ. It is Christ who provides forgiveness of sins and eternal life.

The Bible Is a Guide for Holy Living

To Timothy, his young son in the ministry, Paul wrote, "From a child thou hast known the holy scriptures, which are able to make thee wise unto salvation through faith which is in Christ Jesus" (2 Tim. 3:15). The Psalmist wrote, "How can a young man keep his way pure? By guarding it according to thy word" (Ps. 119:9, RSV). He continues, "I have laid up thy word in my heart, that I might not sin against thee" (v. 11, RSV).

The Bible Is Final and Complete

It says of itself, "If any man shall add unto these things, God shall add unto him the plagues that are written in this book: and if any man shall take away from the words of the book of this prophecy, God shall take away his part out of the book of life, and out of the holy city, and from the things which are written in this book" (Rev. 22:18-19).

WHAT OUR CHURCH BELIEVES
ABOUT THE BIBLE

In keeping with what the Bible says about itself, the Church of the Nazarene believes the Scriptures to be divinely inspired— God's Word given to mankind. Thus the Bible communicates the will of God to the human family. The Article of Faith discussing the Bible found in the *Manual* says:

> We believe in the plenary inspiration of the Holy Scriptures, by which we understand the 66 books of the Old and New Testaments, given by divine inspiration, inerrantly revealing the will of God concerning us in all things necessary to our salvation, so that whatever is not contained therein is not to be enjoined as an article of faith (*Manual*, par. 4).

The Authority of Scripture

Divine inspiration means that the Bible writers wrote the thoughts of God as they were guided by the Holy Spirit. Thus, what the Bible says is true. The term *plenary* (pronounced "*plee*-na-ry" or "*plenn*-a-ry") means full, complete, and entire. One Bible scholar explained that *plenary* means that the Scriptures are absolute, final, and all-sufficient in matters of faith. The word implies the highest possible degree of inspiration but does not require belief in any particular method of inspiration. We hold that the Bible is the authoritative guide for the individual Christian and for the corporate life of the Church. We believe the Scriptures make God's will known to all.

Purpose of Scripture

The Bible is the communication channel God uses to make himself known to us. The Article of Faith states the purpose of Scripture as "revealing the will of God concerning us in all things necessary to our salvation." Though written by many writers over a period of 1,500 years, the main message of the Bible is the salvation of man. The Bible was never planned to be an authority on history or science. God's purpose for His Word is to make His will known in all things necessary to salvation and Christian living. Through the Holy Scriptures, He gives us knowledge and guidance for living meaningful, Christ-centered lives. As we read the Bible with an obedient attitude, the Holy Spirit enables us to understand it and to apply its teachings to our lives.

Organization of Scripture

Although bound in one volume, the Bible consists of 66 books organized into two great divisions, the Old and New Testaments. These books vary in length, authorship, style, and date of writing. *Testament* means covenant or promise between God and man. So the Old Testament is a record of God's promise to the human family before the coming of Christ. And the New Testament is the commitment of God to man completed in the life, death, resurrection, and ascension of Jesus.

The Old Testament consists of 39 books arranged into five divisions:

Pentateuch or Law:	Genesis, Exodus, Leviticus, Numbers, Deuteronomy
Historical:	Joshua, Judges, Ruth, 1 and 2 Samuel, 1 and 2 Kings, 1 and 2 Chronicles, Ezra, Nehemiah, Esther
Poetic and Wisdom:	Job, Psalms, Proverbs, Ecclesiastes, Song of Solomon
Major Prophets:	Isaiah, Jeremiah, Lamentations, Ezekiel, Daniel
Minor Prophets:	Hosea, Joel, Amos, Obadiah, Jonah, Micah, Nahum, Habakkuk, Zephaniah, Haggai, Zechariah, Malachi

The New Testament consists of 27 books divided into four major divisions:

Historical: Matthew, Mark, Luke, John, Acts of the Apostles

Letters of Paul: Romans, 1 and 2 Corinthians, Galatians, Ephesians, Philippians, Colossians, 1 and 2 Thessalonians, 1 and 2 Timothy, Titus, Philemon

General Epistles: Hebrews, James, 1 and 2 Peter, 1, 2, and 3 John, Jude

Prophecy: Revelation

The relationships of the Old and New Testaments center in the ministry of Jesus Christ. The Old Testament is an incomplete book because it looks ahead to Christ. But the New Testament cannot be understood without the foundations of the Old Testament. This dependence is seen in the first chapter of Matthew and continues through 263 direct Old Testament quotations that are found in the New Testament. In addition to these direct quotations, some Bible teachers calculate there are an additional 1,300 allusions or references to the Old Testament found in the New Testament. W. T. Purkiser summarizes the relationship, "The Old Testament is the necessary foundation for the New Testament, and the New Testament is the crown and completion of the Old Testament."[1]

Miracle of Scripture

Ralph Earle has a magnificent statement about the miracle of the Bible. He says, "Though written by many men over a period of a millennium and a half, it has a single message throughout—divine redemption. From Genesis to Revelation it says that man has sinned, a holy God cannot condone sin, but God's love guarantees that He will forgive those who turn to Him in repentance and faith. And that message comes through today just as clearly as it did nearly 2,000 years ago."[2]

INSIGHTS TO DEVELOP BIBLICAL UNDERSTANDING

Have you ever wondered why some people complain that they cannot understand the Bible? Many of these problems grow out of misunderstandings about Scripture itself and about how to use it.

A Profoundly Simple Book

Some Christians talk about the big words in the Bible and the passages that are hard to understand. And some preachers talk about the difficulty of understanding Greek and Hebrew, which were the original languages in which the Scriptures were written. Other Christians find the Bible hard to comprehend because they start their study with one of the more difficult books. They begin in Matthew, for example, and run into that long list of "begats." Or their first encounter may be with the complex Book of Revelation.

It is true. The Bible *is* profound. It is so inexhaustible that even the lifelong student of the Scriptures discovers something new nearly every time he reads it. This miraculous Book keeps leading us to deeper understandings of God and His purposes for us.

But it is also simple. Even the first-time reader discovers that the Bible speaks significantly to him. Thus every Christian, from the new convert to the veteran saint, will find help in the Scriptures. But the Bible must be read if one is to discover its meaning. This least-read best-seller must become the well-read companion of the Christian.

Obedience Produces Understanding

Ordinary books are read and studied for pleasure, for instruction, for information, or even for developing a skill. Too often, students and scholars study the Bible as they would any great historical book. But for the Christian, the Bible is a special kind of book, given to us by God so that we might discover His will and way for us.

If we would understand the Bible's message, we must first

recognize our need for divine help. To comprehend the Scriptures requires a humble spirit, an open heart, and an eager mental attitude. As we become teachable before the Word, we find its application to our personal situation. God opens its meaning to trusting hearts.

The Bible has spoken meaningfully to multiplied generations. Centuries have tested its message, and everywhere that it has been read with submissive faith, it has revived genuine religion. It is thus more than an ordinary piece of writing. It is a special Book that must be reverenced and obeyed. Our coming to the Word of God always goes better when we begin with the Psalmist's prayer, "Open thou mine eyes, that I may behold wondrous things out of thy law" (Ps. 119:18).

How to Get the Most out of the Bible

The Bible is a light to our path, but we must do the walking. God communicates His will to us through these 66 books that make up the greatest Book of all time. Jesus said that we must love God with all our heart, soul, strength, and mind, and that is also the way we must approach our study of His Word. Here are some practical pointers.

1. *Study alone and in groups.* The Bible may be studied in private without discussion with others and even without the aid of such helps as commentaries, dictionaries, or concordances. But the Scriptures often come alive much more quickly when we are in fellowship with other believers and profit by their insights. Also, the deeper things of God come to us more readily with the help of devout Bible teachers and writers.

John Wesley once received a note informing him, "The Lord has told me to tell you that He doesn't need your booklearning, your Greek, and your Hebrew." Wesley wrote back, "Thank you, sir. I already knew the Lord had no need for my 'book-learning,' as you put it. However—although the Lord has not directed me to say so—on my own responsibility I would like to say to you that the Lord does not need your ignorance, either."[3]

God does not need study groups or books on the Bible to communicate the essential elements of faith and meaning to us. But He often uses these helps to enrich our understanding.

2. *Listen to Bible preaching.* Hearing a sermon well is just as important as preaching one well. The communication process is a lot like the noise of a falling tree in a remote forest. While it can be argued that the tree made a great crashing sound when it was blown down, if no one heard it, no knowledge of it was communicated. An unheard sermon is an unheeded sermon.

Real hearing of the sermon is more than courteous listening. Effective hearing means that the listener keeps thinking about the biblical content of the message during the following days and even weeks. He may go back and read the scriptural basis for the sermon again. Sometimes he may ask the preacher for a word of clarification. And the true hearer applies the sermon to his personal situation in an effort to develop a more Christ-centered life. This kind of hearing of the proclaimed Word of God makes the listener and the preacher love-slaves of the Scriptures.

3. *Attend Sunday School.* Do you wish to store up promises against the pressures of life? Do you want to learn more about the Bible? Then get into a Sunday School class where Bible content is taught and applied to real-life situations. Here the Bible is the Textbook and here its truths are explored.

4. *Cultivate a Berean attitude.* When Paul preached to the Christians at Berea, "they received the message with great eagerness and examined the Scriptures every day to see if what Paul said was true" (Acts 17:11, NIV). Such an attitude will make the Bible come alive.

Because it is God's Word to us, the Bible deserves an increasing place of prominence in the preaching and teaching ministries of the church. But the growing Christian, on his own, must keep developing his understanding of the Scriptures on a regular basis.

The Bible Clarifies Our Perspective

Because contemporary life seems to magnify the importance of social acceptance and earthly success, our whole way of looking at life becomes easily distorted and worldly. We are too easily drawn away from stable, spiritual living by the secular voices that keep calling us. But regular Bible reading draws us back to basic values. Our time in the Scriptures helps us to see life as it really is;

the fantasies of the world show up as counterfeit. As we apply the Scriptures to life, genuine spiritual values come clearly to mind. God puts a strength and serenity into life through our frequent contacts with the Bible.

TRANSLATIONS—BANE OR BLESSING

The beauty of the 380-year-old English of the King James Version, first published in 1611, makes it the well-known, much-loved, and often-used version of thousands of serious Christians. It will remain the first choice Bible version for many believers for long years to come.

But the meaning of many words has changed in these 380 years. Also, many manuscripts closer to the originals have been found since the King James translation was made. Thus the new translations would be expected to give more accurately the meaning the original writers intended to convey.

Frequently these days, as the preacher or Bible teacher begins to read from the Scriptures, he announces what translation he is using, giving its "code letters"—KJV, NIV, RSV, NEB, TLB, NASB, NBV, or whatever. Some have laughingly referred to this as "alphabet soup" because there have been so many new translations in recent years. Confusion grows when the listener tries to follow along in his Bible translation when it is a different version from that which the speaker is using. The words are often different and that can be confusing. But the ideas are the same. Thus what appears to be a problem may become a rich diversity that forces the listener to think more about the meaning of the passage rather than listen to mere words.

The purpose of new translations, whatever the century of their origin, is to make the Bible understood in the common language of the people. The original language of the New Testament was the language of the common people—the soldier, the butcher, the housewife, the neighborhood shopkeeper, and the child. So it is appropriate and desirable to translate the Bible that was originally written in everyday Hebrew and Greek into everyday English. Our goal is to make the Bible understandable and available to everyone, including the common man.

There is a distinct possibility that the beautiful words from another era do not startle, condemn, and thrill us as God meant them to do. So since the Bible is God's communication channel to man, it must be read in a translation that most accurately conveys to the reader in his language what God said in the original writing.

The Church of the Nazarene has not officially endorsed any one of the contemporary translations. Nearly every version offers helpful insights into the meaning of various passages. For private study, it may be a good practice to have the King James Version and a newer translation side by side for convenient comparison. Some special printings of the New Testament have several versions in parallel columns.

The difference between paraphrases and translations of the Bible also needs to be understood. For example, *The Living Bible* and the Phillips translation are paraphrases of the Scriptures, which means they are not word-for-word translations, but the ideas are put in modern thought forms. They provide useful devotional material but pose some serious problems when the precise meaning of doctrinal passages is desired. Versions that have been translated from the original languages by groups of Bible authorities rather than individuals are more likely to avoid the problem of personal prejudices and doctrinal slants. Among these are the *American Standard Version,* the *New English Bible,* the *Revised Standard Version,* the *New International Version,* and the *New American Standard Bible.*

Some Christians read a different translation of the Scripture each year in their private devotions to provide an increasing knowledge of God's Word. In Bible classes, study groups, and midweek prayer services, it might be helpful to share the way several translations state a scriptural truth. But for public services of worship and evangelism, our preachers probably serve us best by using the translation that most precisely and powerfully states God's truth to us.

In our study of the Bible, our big purpose is to try to understand accurately what God is saying to us.

How to Enjoy the Bible

Unfortunately, many Christians think the Bible is a dull, uninteresting book. They may read a fragment of it every day through a sense of duty, but they would rather spend time reading a novel, a newspaper, or a magazine.

Many others, however, find the Bible to be a fascinating book. It speaks to their spiritual needs. They could not do without its sustaining influence on their lives.

What is the difference? How can one find real enjoyment in Bible reading and study? How does one move from this sense of duty to a delightful anticipation of time spent in the Bible?

Be in Right Relationship with God

One whose heart is cluttered with sin, who neglects spiritual responsibility, or harbors resentments is out of tune with the Scriptures. The personal knowledge of sins forgiven opens our ears to hear what God is saying to us through His Word. Usually the assurance of personal, present victory encourages a deeper desire to study the Bible and to be open to its truths.

Read at the Level of Your Present Understanding

The Bible was planned by God to nourish us spiritually. The banquet table is not the time for questioning the cook; it is a time to enjoy the food. Obedience and openness are the two keys that move the Christian to deeper levels of scriptural understanding.

Every Christian, at whatever level of Bible knowledge and Christian experience, can find help from Bible reading. Of course, questions will arise sometimes, but as one poetic soul put it, we do not need to understand the wind in order to fly a kite. As we apply the Scriptures to our lives, we start at the level of our present understanding and keep on discovering the deeper things of God. New treasures of spiritual insight will be revealed by repeated readings.

Beginners in Bible study should remember that since the Bible is a library, one does not necessarily start at the beginning and read straight through. So it is wise for them to browse around in this library of 66 books until they see a title that interests them. Just as we might ask a librarian for guidance, they might ask the pastor or Sunday School teacher where to begin.

A possible list for the person who is new to the Bible might be to start with Matthew 5—7 (the Sermon on the Mount); Psalms 23, 24, 100, 122, 139; Isaiah 35, 55; the Gospels of Mark and Luke; or Paul's letter to the Philippians. Then one might turn to one of the Old Testament prophets such as Jeremiah, Amos, Hosea, or Micah. Next, turn back to the New Testament to the Acts of the Apostles. After having completed these sections the reader should be ready to make his own choices.

Take Time

Most believers have some guilt feelings about their use of time. In fact, nearly all of us need to evaluate our schedules. Most of us think we are busy. All of us wish we had more time for Christian service, family togetherness, and Bible reading. But every worthwhile pursuit in life takes time.

Perhaps it would be useful to rethink our use of time. For example, what about the time spent watching TV or reading the newspaper? All relationships in life are enriched when we give ample time to our devotional lives. Life goes better when Bible reading is given an adequate and regular place in our schedules.

Most of us have heard about saints in other generations who have read the Bible for two, three, or more hours per day. Certain stalwart Christians arose as early as 3 A.M. to read the Bible. Others may have read all night. But such examples cannot become exact patterns for us to follow. The important fact to learn is that the cultivation of the spiritual life takes quality time in Bible reading. We might do better to spend 15 prime minutes in the Bible each day than to have a sporadic spurt of an hour or so once a week.

Read Expectantly

We receive more when we expect more. This is a well-known principle of relationships and learning. When you meet a new person, your expectation largely determines whether this person will be a friend or a mere acquaintance. When the student goes into a new class, his expectation will often determine whether the class is interesting or dull to him. When a Christian goes to church, his expectation largely determines whether the service will be inspiring or routine.

Likewise, when the Christian goes to the Bible with the expectation that God will speak to him through the Scriptures, he usually hears from God. His truth is on every page, but it communicates to us only as we are receptive to its message.

For those out of tune with God, the Bible brings a message of conviction. After reading the Bible, one early-teen girl said, "I wish God wouldn't follow me around all the time." But open-hearted reading of the Scriptures gives us new insights that are to be welcomed. Receptivity is increased when we read with thanksgiving for new truth.

Read in Spite of Your Moods

Every human being is affected at times by his moods. Often without any apparent explanation, we experience feelings of high emotion or deep discouragement. One of the biggest lies of the enemy is to tell Christians that their relationship to Christ is determined by their moods. It simply is not true. Our relationship with Christ is based on forgiveness and faith. Read the Bible when you feel like it. Read when you do not feel like it. Read when you seem to have no feelings at all.

Bible reading will frequently lift you above your negative moods with its assurance of God's care. The knowledge that God still lives and provides for us is a great source of blessing guaranteed to change discouragement to song.

Share It

Both the receiver and the giver are enriched by the effort; all are helped by a fresh word from God. Home Bible studies, Sunday School classes, family devotional periods, and even casual conversation all give us opportunities to encourage others with a Bible promise. Often this simple sharing provides a lift for the person to whom we speak and it also keeps us thinking about the passage for longer periods of time.

❧ Read Until It Speaks to You

While setting a goal of reading 10 verses, 2 chapters, or a whole book at one sitting may sometimes be desirable, it is important that you read until the Bible speaks significantly to you. The idea is not to cover a certain number of verses to fulfill a duty but to hear a fresh word from God.

Keep Reading in Spite of Difficult Passages

There will be some sections that you simply do not comprehend. Spurgeon had advice for a new Christian who said he stopped reading the Bible because he came to a part he did not understand. The great preacher said, "When I am eating fish and come upon a bone, I don't fling the whole fish away. I put the bone on the side of the plate and leave it. I go on enjoying the fish."

METHODS OF BIBLE STUDY

In studying the Bible, God does not require brilliance but faithfulness. Instead of adopting some meaningful plan of Bible study, too many Christians use a hit-or-miss method that gives them little information or inspiration.

Bible study should always begin with the assumption that the basic unit of study material in the Bible is the paragraph. A paragraph is a group of related sentences dealing with one central idea. In the KJV these sections are marked with the paragraph symbol (¶). In the newer translations, regular paragraphing or headings are used. Though there are many great individual verses, it is profitable to study them in the context of the surrounding verses.

"I Was There" Study

This method simply means that the reader looks at the biblical record through the eyes of the persons who were there at the time it was written. How did it seem to Lazarus as he came from the tomb tearing aside those graveclothes? How would it be to travel with Jesus and to rub shoulders with Peter, James, and John? As you read Jeremiah, how did his troubled times look to him? How would it have felt to be in prison with Paul? Or what emotion was experienced by the leper when Jesus cleansed him?

As an example, climb into the tree with Zacchaeus to get a better view of Jesus. With a little imagination, every detail becomes vivid. You see the crowd, feel the burning heat, grip the tree limb, almost sneeze in the swirling dust. Then you melt with devotion as Jesus calls your name and invites himself to your home for dinner.

SMA Study Method

This approach simply asks three questions of every passage we read. What does it *say?* What does it *mean?* How can it be *applied* to my life? (S=Say; M=Mean; A=Apply.)

Paraphrase Method

As you read, say to yourself, "What does the passage say to me?" To be most effective, this method requires that a paraphrase of the passage be written. Some people keep a Bible notebook or journal where they write such paraphrases and jot down new insights that come to them as they read. To read the sentence or paragraph over again in your own words will help you retain the understanding you have received from the Scriptures.

Six Question Method

This method is built around the five "Ws" and one "H" formula of the news reporter. Rudyard Kipling put the idea in poetic form when he wrote:

> *I have six faithful serving men,*
> *Who taught me all I know:*
> *Their names are What and Where and When*
> *And How and Why and Who.*

Ask the passage what, where, when, how, why, and who.

Character Studies

Historical characters can best be understood when one charts the forces at work in their lives. One approach would be to use the following guideposts:

- Character influences
- Positive qualities
- Faults and sins
- Great crises
- Major lessons taught
- Relation to the Bible book being studied

Outline

Every Bible book has a central theme that can be discovered by a thorough reading of the book and a study of commentaries. By starting with the major idea of the book, one can then outline each chapter as it relates to this major theme. This same approach can be used in the study of some individual chapters in the Bible such as the theme of "love" in 1 Corinthians 13, "faith" in Hebrews 11, and "abiding" in John 15.

Get the Overview

While it is useful to study details of the Bible, it is also helpful to occasionally read long passages at one sitting. Without interruption, try reading all of Mark's Gospel, all of Acts, or all of Philippians. Any one of these books would make a delightful evening of reading, particularly if a contemporary translation is used. This study of a longer passage will help to develop a comprehensive view of the book.

TOOLS FOR BIBLE STUDY

Every serious student of the Scriptures should have six basic tools:

- Several English Bible translations with paragraph divisions
- English dictionary. Often a passage of Scripture takes on

brand-new meaning when one checks the precise meaning of a word that is used in the passage.

- Bible concordance. A concordance lists all the biblical words and where they are found.
- Bible dictionary. A Bible dictionary defines biblical words that may not be sufficiently discussed in English dictionaries.
- Bible atlas. A Bible atlas is like a road map to help us understand the topography and geography of the Bible.
- Commentaries. A Bible commentary helps the Bible student understand the central idea of the book, the writer's purpose, and the writer's style. A commentary will also provide an outline of the book and offer helpful insights regarding difficult passages.

* * *

Eric Jackson discovered that following the directions for Christian living as found in the Scriptures really gave meaning to his newfound faith. One of his Christian friends told him this story that just seemed to click.

A military plane was reported missing and finally it was presumed down. The official report read, "Lost in the fog." One of the commanders was asked by a news reporter to explain how that could happen with today's sophisticated equipment.

The commander replied, "In going through a fog, a pilot often suddenly loses his sense of direction. Instead of trusting his instruments, he tries to feel or reason his way out of the fog. Before he knows it he is completely confused and it is often too late to recover."

Jackson thought of the application of this story to his own spiritual life. He tried to reason and feel his way out of his spiritual fog. It was almost too late before he turned to the Scriptures, which gave him clear instructions for his new life in Christ.

May God himself,
the God of peace,
sanctify you
through and through.
May your whole spirit,
soul and body
be kept blameless
at the coming of
our Lord Jesus Christ.

1 THESS. 5:23, NIV

Discovering Christian Holiness

ALBERT F. HARPER

Caroline testifies: "It is surprising how blind a person can be even with 20/20 vision. There I stood looking directly at the envelope on my desk, but I couldn't see it. I don't know how long I hunted for it, but I know it was longer than necessary. That's the way it was with my spiritual life.

"As a young adult I realized the great need of my soul for a Savior. Although my life seemed together, it was apart. I could not ignore the longing in my empty spirit. Then He came! Jesus came into my heart, and forgave my sins. I was in His presence, but I still couldn't truly see Him.

"I spent years searching for God's grace that would give me full release from the sin of a double mind and a divided heart. I searched the Scriptures, and they left me craving more. I searched at revival services and in camp meetings. Even in the presence of all that glory, I still could not see.

"And then, having asked the Holy Spirit to remove the blindness of my soul, light was given. I saw myself as He saw me. The sight was not pleasant. It revealed a sinful nature pulling me from the Christ I longed to serve completely. I saw the rotten attitudes

---

ALBERT F. HARPER is former editor in chief, Department of Church Schools; now retired.

that cluttered the heart I wanted to be clean. I saw the selfishness that clogged the spirit that I wanted to be free.

"But as my eyes began to see these barriers clearly, I opened my heart to the Holy Spirit's work—and He gave my soul 20/20 vision! I can now see beyond myself. I see His face—and His reflection is slowly becoming mine.

"Spiritual blindness almost drained my spirit of every beautiful plan God has for my life. But now I am thankful my soul can sing with multitudes who have gone before, 'I once was blind, but now I see'—because of His amazing grace!"

*   *   *

I am glad this young mother attended a church where she learned about holiness. I am glad that she read her Bible and discovered Paul's prayer: "May God himself, the God of peace, sanctify you through and through. May your whole spirit, soul and body be kept blameless at the coming of our Lord Jesus Christ. The one who calls you is faithful and he will do it" (1 Thess. 5:23-24, NIV). I rejoice that the truth of entire sanctification disturbed her until she was not content to continue in a life of division and defeat. I am glad God has given us His grace of Christian holiness.

WHAT IS CHRISTIAN HOLINESS?

Holiness is a grace because it is one of God's gifts to us. But how are we to understand its meaning? To be holy is to be Christlike in spirit. To be holy is to be morally like the God whom we love and serve—to have His spirit and His attitudes. To be holy is to be like God—dead set against every kind of sin. To be holy is to be like God in having my intentions and attitudes motivated by His spirit of love.

To be holy is to be whole, as God intends His child to be. God's purpose for every man and woman is that our lives shall be rich and fulfilled. We find this completeness and satisfaction only as we allow Him to mold our attitudes and actions.

Because He loves us, God says, "Ye shall be holy." Because He wants to make us like himself, He says, "Ye shall be holy; for I am holy."

What the Bible Teaches About Holiness

Old Testament Teaching

Because God wants to give us something of His own holy character, He tells us about it in the Scriptures. Early in the Old Testament He reveals His plan for those who are His people: "I am the Lord your God: ye shall therefore sanctify yourselves, and ye shall be holy; for I am holy" (Lev. 11:44). From this point on, the message of scriptural holiness comes through clearly.

To Israel God promised, "Then will I sprinkle clean water upon you, and ye shall be clean: from all your filthiness . . . will I cleanse you. . . . I will put my spirit within you, and cause you to walk in my statutes, and ye shall keep my judgments, and do them" (Ezek. 36:25, 27). Such a holy heart is a gift from God.

In the face of his outbroken sin, David knew that he needed help from God that went beyond forgiveness for his sinful acts. He prayed: "Hide thy face from my sins, and blot out all mine iniquities. Create in me a clean heart, O God; and renew a right spirit within me" (Ps. 51:9-10).

The Teachings of Jesus

God offers His gift of a cleansed spirit because fallen man has a deep need. Jesus knew that evil deeds arise from an evil condition in the depraved human spirit. He tells us, "From within, out of men's hearts, come evil thoughts, sexual immorality, theft, murder, adultery, greed, malice, deceit, lewdness, envy, slander, arrogance and folly. All these evils come from inside and make a man 'unclean'" (Mark 7:21-23, NIV).

The Bible teaches that it is necessary to have our carnal spirits cleaned up if we are to be Christlike. Jesus tells us that this inner purity is the preparation for fellowship with the Heavenly

Father: "Blessed are the pure in heart, for they shall see God" (Matt. 5:8).

The Scriptures also show us that heart-cleansing is given to us through the work of God's Holy Spirit. John the Baptist declared, "I baptize you with water for repentance. But after me will come one who is more powerful than I . . . He will baptize you with the Holy Spirit and with fire" (Matt. 3:11, NIV).

To do the whole will of God, we need to be filled with the Holy Spirit—and God yearns to meet our need. Jesus said, "If you then, though you are evil, know how to give good gifts to your children, how much more will your Father in heaven give the Holy Spirit to those who ask him!" (Luke 11:13, NIV).

To His early followers Jesus promised: "I will pray the Father, and he shall give you another Comforter, that he may abide with you for ever; even the Spirit of truth" (John 14:16-17*a*). A little later that same evening Jesus prayed to the Father: "I pray not that thou shouldest take them out of the world, but that thou shouldest keep them from the evil. They are not of the world, even as I am not of the world. Sanctify them through thy truth: thy word is truth" (John 17:15-17).

Jesus prayed that we might be sanctified by the cleansing Holy Spirit, but He makes it clear that we must fulfill the conditions for His coming: "Behold, I send the promise of my Father upon you: but tarry ye . . . until ye be endued with power from on high" (Luke 24:49).

Describing these instructions in another place, Luke writes of Jesus' directive, "Do not leave Jerusalem, but wait for the gift my Father promised, which you have heard me speak about. For John baptized with water, but in a few days you will be baptized with the Holy Spirit" (Acts 1:4-5, NIV).

At this time Jesus also explained why it was so important to Him that His followers tarry until they were baptized with the Holy Spirit: "You will receive power when the Holy Spirit comes on you; and you will be my witnesses in Jerusalem, and in all Judea and Samaria, and to the ends of the earth" (Acts 1:8, NIV).

These early followers obeyed Jesus' instructions, and His promise was fulfilled in their lives. "When the day of Pentecost came, they were all together in one place. Suddenly . . . all of them were filled with the Holy Spirit and began to speak in other tongues as the Spirit enabled them" (Acts 2:1-2, 4, NIV). Utterly amazed, the people who heard them asked, "How is it that each of us hears them ... declaring the wonders of God in our own tongues!" (Acts 2:8, 11, NIV).

The Testimony of the Apostles

The gift of the sanctifying Spirit did not cease with the Day of Pentecost. Later when men were converted in Samaria, Peter and John came from Jerusalem. They themselves had received the Holy Spirit in the Upper Room on the Day of Pentecost. When they arrived in Samaria they prayed for the new Christians "that they might receive the Holy Spirit, because the Holy Spirit had not yet come upon any of them; they had simply been baptized into the name of the Lord Jesus. Then Peter and John placed their hands on them, and they received the Holy Spirit" (Acts 8:15-17, NIV).

Saul of Tarsus met Christ on the road to Damascus. Chastened, and open to God's work in his spirit, he prayed in the house of Judas on Straight Street. There, a Spirit-led Ananias came to him and said, "'Brother Saul, the Lord—Jesus, who appeared to you on the road as you were coming here—has sent me so that you may see again and be filled with the Holy Spirit.' Immediately, something like scales fell from Saul's eyes, and he could see again" (Acts 9:17-18, NIV).

Seventeen years later the Lord's man was still proclaiming this uttermost salvation. When Paul found a small group of believers in Ephesus, his first question to them was, "Have ye received the Holy Ghost since ye believed?" They replied, "We have not so much as heard whether there be any Holy Ghost." To these sincere but untaught disciples Paul explained the connection between salvation and Christ's promise of the Holy Spirit. The Bible reports, "When they heard this, they were baptized in the name of the Lord Jesus. And when Paul had laid his hands on them, the Holy Ghost came upon them" (Acts 19:5-6).

Three years still later the missionary writes to his Christian converts in northern Greece, "The very God of peace sanctify you wholly; and I pray God your whole spirit and soul and body be preserved blameless unto the coming of our Lord Jesus Christ.

Faithful is he that calleth you, who also will do it" (1 Thess. 5:23-24).

Stirred by the same concern for God's deeper ministry to His people, James admonishes his Jewish-Christian readers, "Draw nigh to God, and he will draw nigh to you. Cleanse your hands, ye sinners; and purify your hearts, ye double minded" (James 4:8).

John the Beloved was the last living apostle who had known Jesus personally. Remembering the teachings of our Lord, John assures us, "If we walk in the light, as he is in the light . . . the blood of Jesus Christ his Son cleanseth us from all sin. . . . If we confess our sins, he is faithful and just to forgive us our sins, and to cleanse us from all unrighteousness" (1 John 1:7, 9).

The message of Christian holiness thus finds many voices in the Bible. It is clear that a holy God desires a holy people. He makes His will known to us and shows us how we may open our lives to the coming of His Holy Spirit. Early in the Bible we hear God's expressed concern, "Sanctify yourselves, and ye shall be holy; for I am holy" (Lev. 11:44). In a final note from God's written revelation John exhorts the children of God, "Let him who is holy continue to be holy" (Rev. 22:11, NIV).

THE FAITH WE BELIEVE

It is clear that the Bible places great importance on the teaching of holiness. Because that is so, the Church of the Nazarene places great emphasis on this truth. The opening words of the Church Constitution make our position clear:

> In order that we may preserve our God-given heritage, the faith once delivered to the saints, especially the doctrine and experience of entire sanctification as a second work of grace . . . we, the ministers and lay members of the Church of the Nazarene, . . . do hereby ordain, adopt, and set forth as the fundamental law or Constitution of the Church of the Nazarene the Articles of Faith . . .

All 16 Articles of Faith begin with the words "We believe." These are key words, for these doctrines are what we understand to be taught in the Word of God. Bible scholars have arranged these teachings systematically in order to state our doctrines clearly.

Article X gives our teaching on entire sanctification, which is the distinguishing doctrine of the Church of the Nazarene. It is given in two parts, paragraphs 13 and 14. Paragraph 13 reads as follows:

> We believe that entire sanctification is that act of God, subsequent to regeneration, by which believers are made free from original sin, or depravity, and brought into a state of entire devotement to God, and the holy obedience of love made perfect.
>
> It is wrought by the baptism with the Holy Spirit, and comprehends in one experience the cleansing of the heart from sin and the abiding, indwelling presence of the Holy Spirit, empowering the believer for life and service.
>
> Entire sanctification is provided by the blood of Jesus, is wrought instantaneously by faith, preceded by entire consecration; and to this work and state of grace the Holy Spirit bears witness.
>
> This experience is also known by various terms representing its different phases, such as "Christian perfection," "perfect love," "heart purity," "the baptism with the Holy Spirit," "the fullness of the blessing," and "Christian holiness."

Entire Sanctification

We use the term *sanctification* because it is a biblical term; it means "to make holy." We speak of *entire sanctification* because this second work of grace is not God's only action dealing with sin in human life. When our sins are forgiven, God imparts new spiritual life—we call it *regeneration.* We sometimes use the term *initial sanctification* because it is a first work of grace in which God begins to make us like himself.

Entire sanctification comes after we have been forgiven and regenerated. It is the work of God in which He cleanses original sin from the human spirit. Because of the fall of man, we are born into this world with an inclination to sin. It is natural to want our own way. Before self-centeredness has been cleansed, we are inclined to insist on our way even when it conflicts with God's way.

After we have been forgiven, this underlying spirit of wanting our own way is still present in the Christian. No man can do the will of God satisfactorily so long as he harbors a latent spirit of antagonism toward the plans of God. The opposition—every trace of it—needs to be cleansed. A man needs to be sanctified wholly. God promises to do this for us if we will let Him fill us with His own Spirit.

Following Regeneration

We commonly speak of entire sanctification as a second definite work of grace. We believe that this is the way God gives the fullness of His Spirit to us.

In the New Testament the call to holy living is most often addressed to those who are already followers of Christ. Jesus asked His disciples to tarry until the Holy Spirit came upon them. They obeyed Jesus' instructions and were baptized with the Holy Spirit. The apostles' exhortations to be sanctified and to be cleansed were addressed to Christian congregations in the Early Church.

The experience of the Church supports the evidence of Scripture. Almost without exception those who stress the work of the Holy Spirit stress the importance of a conscious seeking for His fullness. Those who testify to an assurance of being filled with the Spirit found this experience and this assurance as a significant crisis after they were converted. These testimonies come not only from within the holiness churches but also from Spirit-filled Christians in other groups.

From our knowledge of human nature we would expect God to deal with us in this sequence. In conversion we are normally thinking about our sins and our need for forgiveness. It is only after we have followed Christ for some time that we sense the need for a deeper relationship. We may discover unexpected attitudes of resistance to God's will. Or, we find ourselves yearning with the songwriter, "Into the love of Jesus, deeper I would go." It is these experiences of conviction and desire that open the door to conscious seeking. At the end of our obedient tarrying we discover a new dimension in our relationship with Christ. It is so outstanding that we can accurately describe it only as a second blessing, *subsequent to regeneration.*

Devotion and Obedience

When the human spirit is cleansed from the sin of opposition, we are *brought into a state of entire devotement to God*. Here is the spirit that Jesus showed in Gethsemane when He prayed, "Father . . . everything is possible for you. Take this cup from me. Yet not what I will, but what you will" (Mark 14:36, NIV). Who can object to such full love for God? Who would find fault with such deep devotion to Christ?

This full acceptance of God's will for our lives is a *holy obedience*. It is an obedience based on *love made perfect*. But it is not an attitude that we can generate by ourselves. Such a spirit flows from a heart filled with God's love; a heart cleansed from self-seeking, and filled with a holy desire to do the whole will of God. This attitude comes from the fulfillment of the divine promise, "I will give you a new heart and put a new spirit in you. . . . I will put my Spirit in you and move you to follow my decrees and be careful to keep my laws" (Ezek. 36:26-27, NIV).

Cleansing and Empowering

To be filled with the Holy Spirit is God's will for us and His gift to us. This is God's work the work of the Father, Son, and Holy Spirit. In the first paragraph of our doctrinal statement we affirm that entire sanctification is an *act of God*. In paragraph three we state that it *is provided by the blood of Jesus*. In the second paragraph we affirm that *it is wrought by the baptism with the Holy Spirit*.

Jesus is our authority for identifying this experience chiefly with the work of the Holy Spirit. Our Lord promised to send the Comforter to His followers, and He told them what the coming of the Holy Spirit would do for them.

We believe that entire sanctification and the baptism with the Holy Spirit are the same work of God. Together they form one experience. When we are filled with the Holy Spirit, His presence cleanses all sin from our hearts. Filled with His love and power, we want nothing contrary to God's will for us. The instantaneous cleansing of entire sanctification is the result of His coming. Also God's indwelling Spirit continues to give strength to overcome evil around us; His presence gives us the desire and the strength to serve our Lord as witnesses.

Several Names—One Reality

We often speak of entire sanctification as the baptism with the Holy Spirit because the Bible uses both terms to describe God's sanctifying work. It is only natural that we should thus find different ways of expressing God's ministry to our spirits. Among Christians we hear God's first work of salvation described in different terms. We speak of being *saved, converted, born again, justified,* and *regenerated.* Human life is beautifully varied, and God's ministries to us affect every aspect of life. It is natural, therefore, to describe His work of entire sanctification as we experience it. That is why we recognize that the reality of this experience may be expressed in different ways.

The terms *Christian perfection* and *perfect love* raise questions even among many who believe in Christian holiness. How can any human be perfect? How can anyone honestly profess that even his love is all that it could be?

The Bible nowhere teaches that we reach a point in Christ-likeness in this life beyond which we cannot improve. By Christian perfection we mean only that it is possible to do what Jesus defined as God's will for us: "Thou shalt love the Lord thy God with all thy heart, and with all thy soul, and with all thy mind" (Matt. 22:37).

It is possible to love God above all else, and in this sense to have a perfect love. It is possible to follow Christ as faithfully as we know how, and in this sense to satisfy Him completely—perfectly. He has given us His own Holy Spirit to inspire and enable us.

Jesus Died to Sanctify Us

Our creed affirms that Jesus died for our sanctification just as truly as He died for the forgiveness of our sins: "Entire sanctification is provided by the blood of Jesus" (par. 13c). The Scripture says, "Wherefore Jesus also, that he might sanctify the people with his own blood, suffered without the gate" (Heb. 13:12). George Bennard reflects the truth of Scripture when he writes,

> For 'twas on that old Cross Jesus suffered and died
> To pardon and sanctify me.

Sanctification Is a Crisis Experience

We believe that God sanctifies us in a moment of time, just as He saves us in an instant. Entire sanctification, like conversion, is thus a crisis experience.

We believe in instantaneous sanctification because that is the way it occurred in the Bible. "Suddenly . . . all of them were filled with the Holy Spirit" (Acts 2:2, 4, NIV). "Then laid they their hands on them, and they received the Holy Ghost" (Acts 8:17).

Sanctification can be an instant experience because faith is the human catalyst that permits the Holy Spirit to unite with our spirits. God's Spirit fills our spirits in a moment of choice—in an act of commitment and trust. In the instant that we exert saving faith, our sins are forgiven. In the moment that we exert sanctifying faith, the Holy Spirit comes in His fullness.

This union with the Spirit of Christ is so complete that Paul sometimes could scarcely determine the boundaries of his own transformed personality. He writes, "I am crucified with Christ: nevertheless I live; yet not I, but Christ liveth in me: and the life which I now live in the flesh I live by the faith of the Son of God, who loved me, and gave himself for me" (Gal. 2:20).

The Place of Consecration

God cannot cleanse our spirits from any attitude that we withhold from Him. He will fill only those areas of our lives that we open to Him. Thus if we wish to be entirely sanctified, we must make an entire consecration. Paul urges, "I plead with you therefore, brethren, by the compassion of God, to present all your faculties to Him as a living and holy sacrifice acceptable to Him . . . And . . . be transformed by the entire renewal of your minds, so that you may learn by experience what God's will is" (Rom. 12:1-2, Weymouth).

We Can Be Sure

When we have made a full consecration, and are trusting God's promise to sanctify us, we may enjoy *the fullness of the blessing.* The *Manual* states our belief at this point: "To this work and state of grace the Holy Spirit bears witness" (par. 13c). We may know when we have been filled with the Spirit and sanctified wholly.

That is the way it happened in the New Testament. Peter knew that he and others had received the promised Holy Spirit on the Day of Pentecost. He had also seen the Holy Spirit given to Gentile converts in Samaria and in the house of Cornelius. When the Holy Spirit comes, He makes His presence known. Peter declares, "God, which knoweth the hearts, bare them witness, giving them the Holy Ghost, even as he did unto us; and put no difference between us and them, purifying their hearts by faith" (Acts 15:8-9).

John Wesley writes: "By the testimony of the Spirit, I mean an inward impression on the soul, whereby the Spirit of God immediately and directly witnesses to my spirit that I am a child of God. The child of God can no more doubt this evidence than he can doubt the shining of the sun while he stands in the full blaze of its beams."

Paul knew this deep inner assurance from God as he wrote, "When we cry, 'Abba! Father!', it is this Spirit testifying along with our own spirit that we are children of God" (Rom. 8:15-16, Moffatt).

A LIFE TO BE LIVED

God's work of entire sanctification begins in a crisis experience. The Holy Spirit comes in His fullness in a moment of time. But the work of that moment in purifying our hearts by faith, is the beginning of a lifelong process of developing mature Christian character.

A holy life is not lived in a moment of time. It takes a lifetime to live a life. But when we have been sanctified wholly we have God's best provision to "serve him without fear in holiness and righteousness . . . all the days of our life" (Luke 1:74-75).

This is the import of paragraph 14 of the *Manual*, which reads:

> We believe that there is a marked distinction between a pure heart and a mature character. The former is obtained in an instant, the result of entire sanctification; the latter is the result of growth in grace.
>
> We believe that the grace of entire sanctification includes the impulse to grow in grace. However, this impulse must be consciously nurtured, and careful attention given to the requisites and processes of spiritual development and improvement in Christlikeness of character and personality. Without such purposeful endeavor one's witness may be impaired and the grace itself frustrated and ultimately lost.

Dealing with Failure

Can a sanctified Christian backslide? Yes. Jesus says clearly, "If a man abide not in me, he is cast forth as a branch, and is withered" (John 15:6). In all spiritual life, what can be received can be lost. It is possible to backslide completely after having been sanctified wholly. Paul warns, "Grieve not the holy Spirit of God" (Eph. 4:30). However, failure usually comes not because of some decisive act of rejection. Rather, there is a gradual, almost unnoticed lack of attention to the spiritual life. Through failure to abide in Christ, we wither.

Carelessness can cause the love of God in our souls to grow weak. When love is weakened, disregard is near. When we disregard God, we may next grieve Him away by blighting indifference or by willful rebellion. The Holy Spirit does not remain where He is not made welcome, nor where His will is rejected.

If after we have been sanctified we become careless of our vows to God, or if we have not been as aggressive in the spiritual life as we should have been, what shall we do? Shall we, in our hours of awakening, throw away our confidence in all that God has done for us? Shall we assume that we are utterly backslidden and are now to begin entirely anew?

No. God is a God of steadfast love. He will not abandon us quickly. But we must cease to be careless or we shall eventually lose our souls. Let us ask God to forgive our neglect. Let us tarry until we are conscious again of His approval and the blessing of His presence. His promise is, "Draw near to God and he will draw near to you" (James 4:8, RSV).

Grow Up into Christ

The goal of the sanctified Christian is Christlikeness. This is an endless quest; no one fully arrives. The various aspects of this growth in holiness are discussed in the following chapter but, in summation, let it be said here that in seeking the goal of Christlikeness one can never be complacent. It involves listening daily to the promptings of the Holy Spirit within. It may require positive effort to do God's will sometimes when we may not particularly feel like it. But for the truly sanctified Christian, to know God's will as the Holy Spirit reveals it, is to do it.

The purpose of Spirit-filled Christians is to live all of life as Christ would want us to live—for as long as we live. Paul voices this longing and commitment for every Spirit-filled Christian: "We will in all things grow up into him who is the Head, that is, Christ. From him the whole body . . . grows and builds itself up in love, as each part does its work" (Eph. 4:15-16, NIV).

My Glad Witness

As a young Christian beginning my junior year in college, I felt a deep need to be cleansed from sin, and to be filled with the Holy Spirit. I knelt at the altar in a college chapel and earnestly sought this blessing. At the altar God graciously dealt with my soul and helped me to reach a place of utter commitment to Him, but the assurance of full salvation did not come immediately. I sought on for a day or two. One morning in my dormitory room as I knelt by the window in meditation and prayer, it happened. Just as the first rays of the rising sun touched the building and lighted up my windowpane, the Holy Spirit came to my soul and illuminated all of my life.

I cannot yet testify to the end of my days, but I can testify that for these years He has been with me. There have been some days of uncertainty, but He has remained faithful. He has made me a better man than I was then. He has led me into paths of Christian service of which I did not dream. The prospect has not always been bright, but looking back the path has always been radiant with the joy of His companionship. In the light of this faith, and with the assurance of His sanctifying presence, I propose to journey until traveling days are done.

*Let us run
with perseverance
the race
marked out
for us.*

HEB. 12:1, NIV

Christians in
the Making

REUBEN WELCH

"I thought I was sanctified; what's gone wrong?" questioned Kelvin Duggin.

After careful attention to preaching on the doctrine of entire sanctification and a thorough search of the Scriptures, Kelvin became convinced of his need for this experience of grace. Following an instructive message on heart purity by his pastor, Kelvin with believing faith consecrated his all to God. True to the scriptural promise, the witness of the Spirit came to him.

For a few days, he felt like a "super saint." But soon the temptation of his old habits of pride and criticism discouraged him. He found that he was frequently pressured by the value system of his friends outside the church. And some of the old resentments seemed to emerge when he thought he was being mistreated. An almost forgotten incident where Kelvin had been wronged by a Christian acquaintance was making it difficult for him to forgive as Christ had forgiven him. His new awareness of his own inadequacy and of his need for much improvement confused Duggin.

How could it be? What was wrong? Kelvin had consecrated his all to God. By faith he had fulfilled the clear instruction of Scripture and believed that he was filled with the Holy Spirit.

REUBEN WELCH is an author, conference preacher, and former chaplain of Point Loma Nazarene College, Pasadena, Calif.

The fact was that nothing was wrong. He was simply learning that sanctified Christians still have a lot of growing to do. And continued obedience to the Word of God made him aware of vast new areas where God wanted him to grow. Kelvin, a sanctified Christian, discovered that he was still a Christian in the making.

"Christians in the making" is not a misnomer, for we use the word *Christian* in more than one way. We use it basically to refer to someone who has believed in Christ, been born again, or saved. But we use it also to describe a person's character or behavior or attitude. In the first use, "Christian" is an accomplished condition. In the second (the sense in which we are using it), it denotes a process that is never fully complete in this world.

THE LIFELONG PROCESS

The making of a Christian in any complete sense is not a simple, immediate act, though it does have a starting point. It is a process both complex and long—lifelong, in fact. The act of becoming a Christian is, of course, a simple, immediate transaction. It happens the moment one is enabled by the Spirit to trust the saving grace of God in Christ for the forgiveness of his sins. It is like the moment of birth, or a moment of rescue, or adoption or reconciliation.

In each of these analogies, however, there is implicit in the very act the reality of process. In other words, the act has no continuing significance apart from the new quality of life that follows. Birth leads to life; rescue means safety; adoption means life in the family, and reconciliation means a new quality of restored relationship. Each of these new conditions fulfills the promise of the initial act. The full potential of that act is reached only as the new condition is worked out over the process of time.

For us, that word *process* is the key word. While it is abundantly clear in the Scriptures that the cleansing, filling, sanctifying work of the Holy Spirit is instantaneous, it is equally clear that crisis is followed by a continuing process. The dot extends into a line, as it were, and what begins in a moment is continued through a lifetime. We need to be careful lest we give so much attention to the instantaneous character of the conversion and sanctification experiences that we neglect the quality of continuing Christian life that is initiated or begun in these crisis experiences.

We must take seriously the progressive aspect of the Christian life. Both the concepts and the vocabulary of growth are essential parts of the Christian life and belong in the working language of the church. Paragraph 25 of the *Manual* states that the objectives of the Church of the Nazarene include not only "the conversion of sinners" and "the entire sanctification of believers" but also "their upbuilding in holiness."

Let us repeat that in our talk about *process* there is no hint of denial of the validity of *crisis.* It is a matter of balance. It is also a matter of obedience to the Word of God. In Hebrews, for instance, believers are shown to be the pilgrim people of God. The process of the race is set before us as surely as is the start and the finish. "Let us run with perseverance the race marked out for us" (12:1, NIV). The process of the race—the long run—is not to be denied but rather affirmed, for it is an essential part of Christian experience.

Because of the developmental aspect of this process phase, it has been called by such terms as *Christian growth, spiritual growth,* or *growth in grace.* To be God's sanctified, developing people we must give earnest attention to both the instantaneous and continuing aspects of the experience.

It is important to keep our thinking about Christian life and growth closely related to our understanding of what sanctification is. After we have been sanctified, we can still talk about growing in the Lord, meeting problems in His strength, overcoming temptation, and finding God's guidance in our lives. In all these things we are, indeed, living out the sanctified life. It means that God, through the work of the Holy Spirit in our lives, is in the process of making us His mature, holy people. Growth and maturity are very much a part of sanctification. So talk about Christians in the making is really talk about the sanctifying work of God in our lives.

THE DIVINE MANDATE

Our growth as Christians is not optional and certainly it is not automatic. There is a great passage in 2 Corinthians that expresses this: "Since we have these promises, beloved, let us cleanse ourselves from every defilement of body and spirit, and make holiness perfect in the fear of God" (7:1, RSV). The verb "make perfect" is in the present tense, which means that it is an ongoing process. We are to be continually at the job of working out holiness in our lives, ridding ourselves of those things that would mar the image of Christ in us.

In Hebrews we are told to leave behind what is elementary and go on to maturity (6:1, RSV). The process of our growing is as much a part of the plan of God in the perfecting of holiness in our lives as is the moment of beginning. It is not just by happenstance; it belongs to the purpose of God for us and cannot be ignored.

Paul tells us in Ephesians 4 that the gifts and ministries are given in the Body so that we may come to "mature manhood, to the measure of the stature of the fulness of Christ; so that we may no longer be children . . . Rather, speaking the truth in love, we are to grow up in every way into him who is the head, into Christ" (vv. 13-15, RSV). How concerned we are these days for the right understanding and exercise of the gifts and ministries in the Body. How clear it is that the purpose of them all is that we grow up. All the process of being together and working together in the Body is tremendously important to God; and so to us.

To the Corinthians, Paul could only speak as to babes (1 Cor. 3:1-2, RSV). Their childishness was expressive of their dependency on the flesh. And what babes we are! It makes me wonder about myself: after all these years I'm not "growed up" yet.

It is needless to pile up the commands and exhortations of Scripture. They are overwhelming when we begin to apply them to our lives. But that is precisely what we must do. In this sense to be a Christian means to be *becoming* more Christian or Christlike.

That is what growth in holiness is. That process is God's work and will in us, but it is no less a command to us. We cannot ignore it.

WE DON'T DO IT OURSELVES

Our concern with growing does not minimize the fact that it is God who sanctifies, both instantaneously and progressively. It is God who works in us as we work out our salvation (Phil. 2:12-13). Everything depends on the fact that God in Christ does for us what we cannot do for ourselves.

God at Work in Us

Sanctification is God's work and the making of Christians, ourselves included, is His work in us. Our part is to believe, to yield, to surrender, to consecrate, to obey. Oh, yes. But all this is also of God. He does the calling, the drawing, the enabling, the cleansing, the filling, and the empowering. It is by faith all the way. In a sense, our growth in grace is really a learning to depend less and less upon ourselves and more and more upon Him. If we keep this vision clear and maintain our balance, we can see more clearly our need for human discipline, human response, human effort without becoming self-sufficient in the process.

Perhaps this is a good place to be reminded that our concern about Christians in the making is not so much for others as for ourselves. The real question here is: What is happening to me? What awareness do I have that God is engaged in a developmental process in my own life through which I become more like Him? We need to *grow*. It is the divine imperative under which we live.

Being Tuned to God's Will

The presence of the Holy Spirit keeps us in tune with the will of God. Jesus promised, "When he, the Spirit of truth, is come, he will guide you into all truth" (John 16:13). Paul describes God's pattern for growth in the sanctified life: "If we live in the Spirit, let us also walk in the Spirit" (Gal. 5:25).

Listening to the voice of the Counselor, we daily discover the will of God for our lives. Following the promptings of the Spirit we walk in the ways that God would have us go. As we do the will of God as it is made known to us, our characters are formed more and more into Christ's likeness.

Entire sanctification is thus not the end of growth in the Christian life. Rather, God's sanctifying Spirit is the stimulus to more rapid growth.

Transformed Desires

It is in the realm of motivation that the Holy Spirit does His principal work. When our hearts are warm with love for God, we are eager to please Him. We listen intently to discern His will, and we act quickly to obey His directions.

When we are sanctified wholly, our love is made perfect. We love God above all others. We put His will above our own. We commit ourselves to follow where He leads, and to do what He commands. We not only *will* to serve Him but also *feel* like it.

Aids for Growth

Can this attitude and this feeling continue? Yes, but not without continuing attention. While the emotions may change, the inner glow of the Spirit's presence can be sustained. It is by the same dedication to God, by the same consuming love, and by the same yearning for Christlikeness that filled our hearts in the early days of our sanctification experience.

How do we consciously nurture our love for God and our commitment to obey His will?

1. By daily fellowship with the Holy Spirit, asking His advice, and listening to His suggestions.

2. By consciously reaffirming our purpose to live Christlike lives.

3. By recognizing and rejecting every temptation to think or act contrary to His suggestions.

What are the requirements for spiritual development?

1. A continuing life in the Spirit.

2. Fellowship with other Christians.

3. Bible reading.

4. Prayer.

5. Some work for Christ through the organized church and with persons in the world.

What are the processes of spiritual development?

1. Thinking daily about our life in Christ.

2. Accepting the impulses to greater Christlikeness that come from our meditation.

3. Watching our daily circumstances to discover what courses of action would be most Christlike.

4. Acting on our impulses and opportunities to do the will of God.

Spiritual growth implies enlargement of spirit. It means doing more than we have done before and venturing into new areas of Christian life and Christian service. The growing edge of the sanctified life is reaching out for more of God and for further expressions of our Christlike concern for persons around us.

Growing in Every Way

Our creed speaks of increasing Christlikeness in *character* and in *personality.* And there is a difference between the two.

Character is the more inward and fundamental concern. Character is what I am, and what God knows my motives to be. Growing in Christian character is the desire and the effort to become more like Christ in my thinking, in the way I feel, in my choices, and in what I do.

Personality is what others perceive me to be. They may be right, or they may be mistaken. It is my Christian job, however, to give them through my behavior the clearest possible reflection of the work God is doing in my spirit. Christ is interested in this reflection of His grace within me because Christian faith is a social religion. God's work goes forward as my friends and associates see Christ at work in me. The Holy Spirit reminds me of the way my attitudes and actions affect other persons.

Growth in Christian personality means that I listen to the voice of the Spirit when He reminds me of how Christ would react toward other persons if He were in my place. Sometimes He commends and encourages me. Sometimes He reproves. In either case I grow when I listen.

TAKING THE WORD SERIOUSLY

Christ's imperative call to holiness demands of us also a new seriousness about the ethical teachings and exhortations of the Scriptures. There are parts of the Bible we take very seriously—those parts that teach about who Jesus is, what He does, how He saves, how He sends His holy, sanctifying Spirit, and how He will come again in glory.

Look at the Book of Romans, for example. It contains just about all the fundamental truths we believe:

- the gospel's connection with the Old Testament
- the deity and humanity of Jesus
- the gospel's power of God for salvation to everyone who believes
- the revelation of God's righteousness and the revelation of His righteous wrath
- the universality of man's fallenness and his willful, helpless sinfulness
- the gracious reality of justification by faith
- our reconciliation through His blood
- the call to die to the old life and a rising to the new
- the call to yield ourselves to God
- our freedom from legalism and from the awesome power of the law of sin and death
- the gracious power of the Spirit for holy living and our hope of eternal glory
- our faith in the saving purposes of God in history, working with Jews and Gentiles to fulfill His gracious will.

"O the depth of the riches and wisdom and knowledge of God!" (Rom. 11:33*a*, RSV).

We really do believe all this! It expresses our understanding of ourselves and our sin and our salvation and our hope for this world and the next. And it is all found in chapters 1 through 11. When we finish with Rom. 12:1-2 we think we are done with the whole book. I am thinking about how many years I have preached and taught the great message in Romans and never got beyond 12:1-2.

But the great ethical teaching of chapters 12—15 brings the marvelous truths of the gospel down into the arena of our daily lives and confronts us with the practical will of God. We are very serious about Rom. 3:23: "All have sinned and fall short of the glory of God" (RSV). But the Spirit also calls us to live in the light of Rom. 12:3. A Christian is "not to think of himself more highly than he ought to think, but to think with sober judgment" (RSV). What a word for us to live by in a society honeycombed with status-seeking and pride! If God's sanctifying work is going on in me, I will have a realistic evaluation of who and what I am in relation to Him.

See how our habit of criticism is brought to the Cross when we give careful thought to the words of 12:10. "Outdo one another in showing honor" (RSV). It sounds like God's remedy for the put-down mentality.

And what of the words of Jesus? I think of the Beatitudes and how they could change our lives if we would receive them as given to us for blessedness in the real world. What of the whole Sermon on the Mount, the parables, the teachings? They are not back there somewhere, they are here, where we are, preserved for us by men who had experienced the sanctifying power of the Holy Spirit and who were learning the meaning of discipleship in that 1st century. To us who are privileged to be Spirit-filled disciples at the close of the 20th century, His words bear the same authority and power.

The examples are endless. The point is that in the process of our maturing, we must give the same careful attention to the ethical exhortations as we do to the call to salvation of which they actually are a part.

ORDINARY HOLY LIVING

For most of the years of my Christian life I have identified becoming more mature principally with becoming more spiritual or more pious. I have thought of Christian growth more in terms of how to pray or how to withdraw and concentrate on holy things and so to be less involved with this earthly, mundane life. I am discovering, however, that the more I turn to the Scriptures and their exhortations to holy living, the more natural, the more human, the more humane, and the more genuine I become. The spiritual movement is not up and away from ordinary living, but up and away from ordinary pretense and pride.

I used to think that the closer to God I was, the farther away I would be from the things of this world. But that could lead to neglect of some basic obligations and ministries. To give more time to prayer and Bible reading and listening to religious programs and going to religious events might mean less time for mowing the lawn or paying the bills or helping a neighbor to start his car or looking for a job. More time spent at church could mean less time to say thank-you to a friend or to ask someone in distress, "What can I do to help?" But it is not an either/or situation. Both aspects are parts of Christian living. The problem is that somehow we have not thought of these ordinary things as part of our life in the Spirit.

Is it really more holy to pray than to care or to listen or to help? Is it more spiritual to read God's Word than to write a letter of encouragement to someone? They are different, but all of them are necessary.

All through the Old Testament the call to be holy as God is holy is related to all sorts of things: How one sacrifices, what one eats, what is not to be touched, how the poor are to be treated, how one's neighbor is to be related to, and how strangers are to be dealt with. Belonging to God affects the whole of life.

Jesus, who "went about doing good," told us that "sheep" and "goats" are separated on the basis of such things as feeding the hungry, clothing the naked, and visiting the sick and imprisoned (Matt. 25:31-46). I'm thinking that it is a serious thing to take the Bible seriously.

There is a sense in which some people try to be more "spiritual" than Jesus. They shy away from the ordinary traffic of life. But Jesus identified himself with the common, everyday things. He rubbed shoulders with all kinds of people. He talked about the kingdom of God in terms of farming and fishing and buying and selling and eating and drinking. The making of a Christian does not mean withdrawal from, but involvement with life.

Strange, isn't it, that spiritual life often seems to express itself in what may appear to be "unspiritual" ways—like how we relate to others, how we handle our emotions, and how responsibly we carry out our duties and honor our commitments. And isn't it significant that Paul would tell us that giving our bodies to God for service is our "spiritual act of worship"? (Rom. 12:1, NIV).

The common life is the only life we have. It is given to us from God, and redeemed by His entrance into it in Jesus. It is the arena of our pilgrimage and the place, the only place, where God's sanctifying work in us is accomplished.

ACCEPTING OUR HUMANITY

The acceptance of our Christian life in the context of the common life leads to our acceptance of ourselves as genuine, human persons. We belong to a fallen race of fellow beings. I believe that part of the process of maturing is the realistic acceptance of our human weaknesses and failures. Our lives in Christ are not lived apart from this world. We need a continuing recognition of our areas of need and of our weaknesses as well as an openness to the illumination and cleansing of the Spirit.

I think of the phrase in Eph. 4:15 (NIV), "Speaking the truth in love, we will . . . grow up." I believe part of that truthful speaking is acknowledging the truth about ourselves—to ourselves, to God, and sometimes to trusted friends. The word of James is fitting here, where he related the healing of sickness to the confession of sins: "Confess your sins to each other and pray for each other so that you may be healed" (5:16, NIV).

We have experienced the initial cleansing work of God's Spirit, but we have a thousand miles to go to become what God wants us to be. We might just as well say yes to that and let our weight down on the real truth. We are simple, human folk who need very much the continuing grace of God in continual forgiveness and cleansing.

Several aspects of our humanness must be taken into account in order to properly understand growth in the Christian life.* First, there is the astonishing depth and complexity of our human personalities. We have life all figured out—and then we turn 21. Suddenly the whole world is different. We no sooner get our heads together on that than we come face-to-face with mid-life crisis. We discover things about ourselves we never knew existed. At various points in this revelation of ourselves, we say in astonishment, "I do get my feelings hurt," or "I really do tend to be a selfish person," or "I am pressured by my senses," or "I'm too conformed to the values of my friends," or "I am struggling with resentment," or "I have never fully forgiven that one who wronged me."

These revelations are part of the Spirit's work within us. They call us to a spirit of repentance and yielding as we walk with the Lord and grow in Him. Full self-knowledge is never made a requisite for entrance into the holy life. Thank God for that!

As we grow, we learn things about ourselves that may confound us, or shame us—maybe even bless us. It is the Spirits ministry. If we wish to grow, we must be willing to face the truth about ourselves, to confess and yield our all to God.

> *Search me, O God, and know my heart!*
> *Try me and know my thoughts!*
> *And see if there be any wicked way in me,*
> *and lead me in the way everlasting!*
>   (Ps. 139:23-24, RSV)

Then there is the tendency among Christians not to fully realize the power of habit. We are bound far more fully than we are aware by our customary ways of doing and thinking. The acceptance of our humanness means the recognition that we are habit people but also that the Holy Spirit can help us break this destructive bondage. Thank God, hindering habit patterns can be changed—not easily, but they *can* be changed. God cares about such things and His Spirit is present in the process of our confessions and repeated commitments of our habit problems to Him.

Again, the acceptance of our humanness means acceptance of the fact that life is always changing. What needless words! We

---

*The author is indebted here to Stephen Neill who, in his book *Christian Holiness*, helpfully discusses these areas in which our humanness impacts our spiritual lives.

see the whole world changing before our very eyes. We cling tightly to the security of the old familiar ways while at the same time we think differently than we used to. We have to admit that old ways of thinking won't do. Ecology, the nuclear arms race, nationalism, instant worldwide communication, the growing gap between the haves and the have-nots—the list never ends. These all impinge upon our thoughts and life-styles. No wonder we cling to old ideas and familiar paths that are not so threatening. The hymn writer, Henry Lyte, speaks to this in these words:

Change and decay in all around I see;
O Thou who changest not, abide with me!

But maturity means the acceptance of the transient, the temporary, the ever-changing character of our human existence. Frightening change calls for a growing trust in the leadership of the God who is changeless. He is also the God of His pilgrim people on their journey. He is always in front of us, urging us to follow Him and to find our security in His changeless love.

Finally, we are reminded that every stage of our lives has its own temptations and potential for failure. We overcome the temptations of youth and middle age, only to find that later years bring new ones of which we had not dreamed. Somewhere along the way we must come to terms with the reality of failure. This includes those failures in ourselves that, incidentally, are the most difficult of all to acknowledge.

But we must know that our human failures do not nullify the grace of God in us. Our refusal to open up and confess them to Him does!

Even those who have a tendency to think that if we are really sanctified we won't have failures, need to understand this. Part of the sanctifying process is learning how to admit and to confess our failures and then to accept the forgiving and continued cleansing power of God. Then we go on our way rejoicing. I've come to believe that the right response to our failures is not, "I thought I was sanctified; what's gone wrong?" Rather, we should humbly say, "Father, what do You want to say to me in all this? I am open to Your voice and I want to obey."

This was the great lesson that Kelvin Duggin needed to learn.

CHRISTLIKENESS—THE GOAL

Some final word needs to be said about the question, What are Christians-in-the-making being made into? The journey has a destination and the process has a purpose.

It is the plain teaching of the Bible that the final goal of it all is likeness to Christ in a holy heaven. "Beloved, we are God's children now; it does not yet appear what we shall be, but we know that when he appears we shall be like him, for we shall see him as he is. And every one who thus hopes in him purifies himself as he is pure" (1 John 3:2-3, RSV). These words make clear to us another, more immediate goal. It is a growing likeness to Christ while we are in this unholy world.

The central objective of all our progress is likeness to Jesus. He is the center of all God's self-revelation and redemptive work.

He answers the question: What is God like?

He answers the question: What is the Holy Spirit like?

And He answers the question: What is the Christian like? To be filled with the Spirit means to know the fullness of the Spirit of Christ. The Spirit-filled life is the Christlike life. The purpose of this ongoing growth in the Spirit is the cleansing away of whatever is unchristlike in us. Growth in holiness is the cultivation of Christlike qualities of heart and life. We are to be like Jesus. It is as simple—and as complex—as that.

We need a new emphasis upon the life and teaching of Jesus. To understand what it means to be holy—what it means to be Spirit-filled, what it means to live the sanctified life—we need to read not only the Book of Acts and the Epistles, but also the Gospels—Matthew, Mark, Luke, and John. Of course, we know that Jesus lived and taught before the coming of the Holy Spirit at Pentecost. But those Spirit-filled disciples are the ones who later gave us the story of Jesus and recorded for us His teachings. Jesus himself had promised that the Spirit would bring to their remembrance all that He had said (John 14:26).

For 25 years and more after Pentecost they preached and taught and catechized and missionized and memorized and shared the story of Jesus—His doings and His teachings. Then they finally wrote down the story for us under the inspiration of the Spirit who had been poured out at Pentecost. So, in this sense, the life and teaching of Jesus do not belong to a pre-Pentecost time. They belong to our present "age of the Spirit."

I believe profoundly that we find in the life and teaching of Jesus all the guidance we need for this new life in the Spirit. Jesus found guidance for himself in obedience to His Father's word and will, as we read in such passages as Matt. 4:1-11; John 5:19, 30; 6:38; 8:28; and 15:10. Even so, we find guidance for our own lives as we are obedient to His Word and will (see Matt. 7:24; John 15:10; 17:7-8). We become Christlike by cherishing His words, receiving them, listening to them, and obeying them as the Holy Spirit brings them to our remembrance.

We are, indeed, Christians-in-the-making. We have a long way to go but the journey is for real and is itself part of God's process. Best of all, God is with us and His Spirit is at work to make Christ central in our lives. This, after all, is the goal.

*I will build
my church, and
the gates of Hades
will not overcome it.*

MATT. 16:18, NIV

Life in the Body of Christ

MELVIN McCULLOUGH

Beverly came through the front door of the church that Wednesday evening for the Bible study as a stranger to the people. She was a newcomer to the community. Her husband, Bob, had accepted a transfer and a new job in the city. The moving van had delivered the family's household belongings.

The new neighborhood was unfamiliar. Old family and social ties were missing. The kids were not sure they would like the schools. There were many decisions to make. Would they ever get settled in the house? The stress was building for Beverly and her family.

When she arrived at church she was carrying a lot of emotions and frustrations. Before the Bible study started the people "circled up" in small groups all over the sanctuary to share their needs and pray for one another. Beverly knew this was especially prepared for her, and she entered into the sharing wholeheartedly. When her circle finished praying, Beverly looked like a different person from the one who only minutes before had come through the doors an anxious stranger. The tensions were released . . . relational warmth was experienced new strength flowed . . . rootlessness was not nearly the problem it had been.

MELVIN McCULLOUGH is pastor of Bethany First Church, Bethany, Okla., formerly executive secretary, Department of Youth, and superintendent of the Washington Pacific District.

When the pastor asked if anyone would like to share some praise, Beverly spoke:

> I am a new Christian. Our family just moved here a week ago and it hasn't been easy for us to make the transition. I've been so lonely I could die. We left our Christian friends and church that meant so much to us ... Don't mind these tears ... I've been asking the Lord all day, "Lead me to some group of believers. I need someone to pray for me and with me." I'm glad I'm here. A really overwhelming need has been satisfied in my life.

No one can read the New Testament carefully and objectively without discovering that God has a unique plan for every Christian during his life on earth. His plan is an eternal one, but that plan impacts space and time. God purposes that you and I be participating members of a local church—a congregation of believers. These fellow Christians care for one another, minister to one another, build up one another in Christ, and then scatter into their world to be the most powerful force on earth for good. There is a desire, a felt need in every follower of Jesus Christ to relate and belong to one another—to be a part of His Church.

What Is the Church?

Our society has a lot of different ideas about the church. The social scientist analyzes the church as one among many human groups that come together in response to certain human needs. The church can thus be viewed as playing a part in society along with schools, hospitals, and the Rotarians. Some think of it as the building at 12th and Main Street.

For many the church is a kind of religious club that one affiliates with like one would with a political party or the local racquet club. Some see it as a waiting room for people expecting to get on board the next bus for heaven. Others approach it as a good place for building their public image and socializing with the "right" people. To be perfectly honest, the church has, in fact, been these things to many people in many places.

But the church did not get started because a few bored people sitting around a table one night decided it would be nice if they had something to do on weekends ... a comfortable place where they could meet once a week. The Church was not man's idea. The Church was Christ's doing.

The concept of the congregation was clearly taught in the Old Testament. It was within this social pattern that God elected to bring forth His Son and in it our Lord chose to worship and work (Luke 4:16). One of the first acts of our Lord's ministry was to establish a community—a small band of 12 disciples to be with Him and work with Him (6:13). Christ declared, "I will build my church, and the gates of Hades [hell] will not overcome it" (Matt. 16:18, NIV). The "stuff" of this building would be those who believed that Christ was the Messiah, the Son of the Living God (v. 16). This new community of the people of God would be built with Jesus Christ as its Cornerstone (Eph. 2:20).

When the New Testament writers speak of the Church it is clear that it consists of those who have experienced the new birth through faith in Jesus Christ. This is essentially what our *Manual* statement says: "The Church of God is composed of all spiritually regenerate persons, whose names are written in heaven" (par. 23). Our relationship to the Church centers first in a Person. It is not first joining some local fellowship, or maintaining a ritual, or expressing social concerns. You join God's family by a life-changing encounter with Jesus Christ. What a family!

The Church is thus a divine-human agency created by God through Christ (Col. 1:18) and empowered by the Holy Spirit (Acts 1:6-8). It consists of persons who have been converted and are seeking to do God's will.

But the Church is also groups of people here and there who have a special relationship with each other. They are bound together in fellowship (koinonia) and are the instruments through which God seeks to draw people in their respective communities to himself. The *Manual* statement in paragraph 24 states our understanding at this point as follows: "The churches severally are to be composed of such regenerate persons as by providential permission, and by the leadings of the Holy Spirit, become associated together for holy fellowship and ministries."

On the Day of Pentecost the community of believers were gathered and the Church came into being by the descent of the Holy Spirit upon them (Acts 2). In the years that followed, this energized Church impacted the whole pagan Roman Empire. The good news on the lips of these disciples crossed the seas and the deserts, traveled to cities and villages, and finally came to the very palace of Rome.

By A.D. 300 the Church had shown such tremendous vitality and was spreading so swiftly that it appeared the entire civilized world would be evangelized. But sad to say, the Church failed to continue to live by clear biblical principles and the world it might have saved slipped into the darkness of the Middle Ages.

Weeds in Good Sod

The weaknesses and failures of the Church are written into the history books along with its successes. Many bad-mouth the Church because they cannot understand why the same institution can on one hand be the source of hypocrisy and on the other be the greatest source of joy and life. But one ought not to be surprised, for Jesus warned that there would be tares amidst the wheat. In an urban setting one could paraphrase His parable by describing the wheat as "good green sod" and the tares "weeds." Jesus said that He would lay beautiful green sod, true Christians, in the fields of the world but at the same time Satan would sow weeds, counterfeit Christians.

If you've ever put new sod down in a yard, you know that in the first few weeks if the soil is properly prepared, and the sod is carefully watered and fertilized it will take root and turn luscious green. For a while you can admire your weedless lawn. But the wind will blow onto your yard the seeds of crabgrass, dandelions, and what not, and those seeds will sprout. There's no way to avoid them. You can guard the grass night and day but the weeds will grow . . . they will grow in the seams of those rolls of new green sod. You can talk to them and threaten but to no avail. Every lawn has its weeds. Our Lord said that the Church would have both good sod and some weeds. He also said there was no point in trying to separate them. The two will grow together until the day of harvest or accountability. The weeds will then be separated and burned up.

Even the New Testament Church had some weeds—Ananias

and Sapphira in Acts 5 and Simon in Acts 8. It was the task of the apostles to set forth the principles that would enable Christians to avoid the false and to be authentic.

A Body and a Family

The New Testament has approximately 30 images to help us understand what the Church is like. Two of these analogies are found in Ephesians where the apostle Paul depicts the Church as a physical body and as a family.

At the end of the first chapter Paul says that the Church is a body. He writes of Christ's Body as "the fulness of him who fills all in all" (Eph. 1:23, RSV). The Church is a living organism; it is part of the life of Jesus Christ present on this earth.

At the close of the second chapter, Paul says the Church is like a family. We are members of "the household of God" (Eph. 2:19). William Barclay translates "household of God" as "family of God." This suggests the most meaningful and intimate relationship. In God's family we are all bound together as brothers and sisters.

The illustration of the Church as a physical body teaches all Christians how important it is for them to be participating members of their churches. The human body has many parts and each has a different function. The feet are not designed for hearing nor are the ears useful in walking. Paul says in Rom. 12:5 that the Body of Christ functions like the human body. Each Christian is a member of the Body of Christ and has a specific function to perform. Every church member is important and has a contribution to make. Are you living up to your full potential as a "foot" or an "ear"?

Being part of a family is something with which most people can identify. A church patterned after the Bible is to be like the family unit. Paul reminds the Roman Christians to "be devoted to one another in brotherly love" (Rom. 12:10, NIV). Here is warmth, tenderness, emotion, concern, and loyalty. As in most families there sometimes are disagreements. But any brother or sister worth his salt would defend his family. Their common heritage binds them together with a devotion to one another.

THE GOAL IS MATURITY

Let's go back to our Bibles for an answer to the question: What does God want to do through the Church? I hope you're ready for it. Read it carefully and thoughtfully. Paul states it this way:

> . . . until we all attain to the unity of the faith, and of the knowledge of the Son of God, to a mature man, to the measure of the stature which belongs to the fulness of Christ. . . . speaking the truth in love, we are to grow up in all aspects into Him, who is the head, even Christ, from whom the whole body, being fitted and held together by that which every joint supplies, according to the proper working of each individual part, causes the growth of the body for the building up of itself in love *(Eph. 4:13, 15-16, NASB)*.

Here's the measuring stick for your life in the family of God. Are you making progress toward maturity? Our Lord wants grown-up followers who are becoming more and more like Jesus Christ. He wants to discover in their lives the fruit of the Spirit—humility, gentleness, patience, and forbearing love (Eph. 4:2). This is the criterion for determining if the Church is fulfilling its supreme purpose.

A SPECIFIC WORSHIPING FELLOWSHIP

One of the unscriptural twists on the contemporary scene is the idea of a "churchless ministry" . . . being a Christian out there in the world without being involved in a specific worshiping community of believers. It is a misnomer, for there can be no church apart from community. Every disciple should realize that he cannot live in isolation. Each should find a group of fellow Christians —a church—where he can be edified and share in witness to the world. The first step in discipleship is not complete until the believer is incorporated into a local church and living as a responsible member of that congregation.

The Scripture commits believers to both the corporate group

idea and the idea of belonging. Jesus called a small band of 12 disciples around Him (Luke 6:13). He talked about His flock (John 10:2-5) and about building "my church" (Matt. 16:18). These are corporate figures of speech. After the birthday of the Church at Pentecost, new followers were incorporated ("added") into the Church daily (Acts 2:47). Thus the Church is to be both personal and collective.

This is the context in which the Church of the Nazarene finds its place in the world. Its role is stated in paragraph 25 of the *Manual* as follows:

> The Church of the Nazarene is composed of those persons who have voluntarily associated themselves together according to the doctrines and polity of said church, and who seek holy Christian fellowship, the conversion of sinners, the entire sanctification of believers, their upbuilding in holiness, and the simplicity and spiritual power manifest in the primitive New Testament Church, together with the preaching of the gospel to every creature.

THE CHURCH AT WORSHIP

Before disciples scatter for ministry it is essential that they gather for worship, instruction and nurture, the breaking of bread, the sacraments, and prayer (Acts 2:42-47).

The Church of the Nazarene, like most other Protestant churches, has two sacraments. A sacrament is an act of worship that Jesus initiated with His followers. The two sacraments are baptism and the Lord's Supper, or Communion. We have already noted that baptism is a way of witnessing to the fact that we have accepted the benefits of the atonement of Jesus Christ through faith. (See chapter 1.) The Lord's Supper is a celebration and remembrance of Christ's sacrificial death for our sins. The significance of Communion and the requirements for participating are stated in the *Manual* as follows:

> We believe that the Memorial and Communion Supper instituted by our Lord and Savior Jesus Christ is essentially a New Testament sacrament, declarative of His sacrificial death, through the merits of which believers have life and salvation and promise of all spiritual blessings in Christ. It is dis-

tinctively for those who are prepared for reverent appreciation of its significance, and by it they show forth the Lord's death till He come again. It being the Communion feast, only those who have faith in Christ and love for the saints should be called to participate therein (par. 17).

Christians place a high priority on worship—every week! Some may say, "I'm tired. That's the only day I get off." But really, folks, that is the only day we have to come together to meet God in the Word, in the great hymns of the Church, and in prayer. The Church is in the world to edify, to be a means of grace to Christians, to minister to the needs of others within the fellowship, and to reach out to the world with the saving message of the gospel.

COME JOIN THE MINISTERIAL ASSOCIATION

Once a disciple is part of the Body and enrolled in the school of spiritual growth, he soon discovers that every member works at what God has given him to do. Every born-again member of the Church has been given at least one spiritual gift (1 Pet. 4:10; 1 Cor. 12:11). These spiritual gifts are given for the purpose of ministry or service (Eph. 4:12).

It is clear, then, that ministry is not just for the pastor or other paid church staff. Every member is placed in the Body of Christ as a ministering member of the Church. This is a "Ministerial Association" not just for the local clergy but for every follower of Christ. Very early in the spiritual journey a disciple should endeavor to discover his gifts (see Romans 12; 1 Corinthians 12; and Ephesians 4) and put them to work in a ministry.

BUILD UP ONE ANOTHER

Ministry begins first to other members of the Body. Paul says that "when each part [of the Body of Christ] is working properly" it results in "bodily growth and upbuilds itself in love" (Eph.

4:16*b*, RSV). There can be no shirkers in the Church if it is to perform its ministry.

The General Rules in the *Manual of the Church of the Nazarene* urge us, among other things, to be "helpful to those who are also of the faith, in love forbearing one another"; "contributing to the support of the ministry and the church and its work in tithes and offerings," and "attending faithfully all . . . the means of grace" (par. 27). Ours is a participating church.

When a church in which there is not love for one another attempts to reach out to the world in evangelism or social action, little is accomplished. When warm Christian fellowship is not displayed among its members, then its witness in the marketplace sounds empty.

The New Testament lays emphasis upon the need for Christians to know each other intimately enough to be able to bear one another's burdens, admonish one another, and minister encouragement to other members of the Body.

When all the 58 "one another" exhortations in the New Testament are studied carefully and grouped together, they can be reduced to 12 significant action ministries that Christians are to perform to help build up the Body of Christ:

1. Be members one of another (Rom. 12:5)
2. Be devoted to one another (Rom. 12:10)
3. Honor one another (Rom. 12:10)
4. Be of the same mind one toward another (Rom. 15:5)
5. Accept one another (Rom. 15:7)
6. Admonish one another (Rom. 15:14)
7. Greet one another (Rom. 16:16)
8. Serve one another (Gal. 5:13)
9. Bear one another's burdens (Gal. 6:2)
10. Bear with one another (Eph. 4:2)
11. Submit to one another (Eph. 5:21)
12. Encourage one another (1 Thess. 5:11)

LOVE ONE ANOTHER

Paul closes his Roman letter by mentioning 26 persons by name—that's an effective way of building up people! He gives an exhortation to "greet one another with an holy kiss." I don't remember hearing a sermon preached on that particular text or a serious treatment of it at seminary. Perhaps it is not culturally relevant! But the principle is there. There are to be tangible expressions of true Christian love that are more than mere social grace. People say, "Hello, how are you?" without any thought of wanting to know how you really are. Our greetings are not to be empty and meaningless but are to be shared with warmth and sincerity communicating our concern for one another. If there are bad feelings and attitudes, they should be confessed. We must be liberated from our resentments. Let's welcome our brothers and sisters in the Lord with open hearts as well as open arms.

In the Early Church a kind of rhythm was evident in which Christians gathered to minister to one another. Then they would scatter into the world to let the glow of their love-filled lives overflow in witness that drew love-starved pagans like the ice-cream wagon draws little children. Pray that you may be the channel for that to happen in the local "body" where you participate.

Great Commission Evangelism

Ultimately discipleship involves spiritual reproduction. When Jesus called His disciples, He informed them that they were to become fishers of men. He used agricultural imagery to explain that sharing the gospel would produce the harvest He wanted. And as part of their training He sent them to various cities to share the Good News.

The climax of their discipleship training came following Jesus' crucifixion and resurrection when He gave them the Great Commission. Just moments before He ascended into heaven He reminded them that they were to be His witnesses to the world. It was their responsibility to go everywhere making disciples. This was the Lord's command to all who would follow Him. His disciples are to produce other disciples.

When the Church was launched on the Day of Pentecost, the disciples became bold witnesses for their Lord. Their spoken witness supported by their radiant lives, their love for each other, and their obedience to their faith was effective in leading thousands of converts to Christ. When persecution forced many of them out of Jerusalem, they witnessed wherever they went. Some of them went to Antioch, a major city in what is now Syria, and established a strong fellowship of believers. It became the church that sent Paul and Barnabas on their first missionary journey. Significantly, that sending came as a result of the Holy Spirit saying to the local congregation, "Set apart for me Barnabas and Saul for the work to which I have called them" (Acts 13:2, NIV).

The disciple-making mission of the Church of the Nazarene follows in the great evangelistic tradition of the Early Church. The general rules for membership in the Church of the Nazarene emphasize the importance of "pressing upon the attention of the unsaved the claims of the gospel, inviting them to the house of the Lord, and trying to compass their salvation." There are various ways to accomplish this mission, including personal evangelism, church revival meetings, and outreach programs designed to bring people under the influence of the gospel.

Every Christian should accept some responsibility in the task of winning people to Jesus Christ. Some disciples will have gifts that make them particularly effective in bringing people to a point of decision for Christ. Others will possess gifts that assist and support the soul-winning ministry of the church. But every follower of Christ will be a witness ready to give testimony to his faith. Every church should diligently train its members in effective ways of sharing their witness and helping others find Christ as Savior.

Whatever else of good the Christ follower is involved in, his service to the Lord is not complete until he is effectively involved in producing new Christians.

A KINGDOM CONSCIOUSNESS

The biblical concept of the Church sees the Church as the community of God's people—a people who live out and witness to the priority of the kingdom of God. The kingdom of God was probably the central message of our Lord's ministry. "He went about all Galilee . . . preaching the gospel of the kingdom" (Matt. 4:23, RSV). To speak of the kingdom of God is to remind ourselves of God's rule and authority over all.

The Church is the agent of God's mission here in the world . . . the agent of the kingdom of God. There is no question that the Church is God's means for accomplishing His work on earth. He made no other provision. Many other organizations and agencies may exist alongside the Church. Some are even helping to support the Church's mission. But they do not take the place of the Church.

Maturing disciples must be sensitized to the Church's responsibility and privilege to be God's agent on behalf of the Kingdom. When this vision grips us, it gives a renewed sense of mission and confidence and we begin to realize that God has big, impressive, and world-shaking plans for us . . . *"immeasurably more"* than anything we could ask or imagine (Eph. 3:20, NIV).

THE CHURCH DEFINES ITSELF

At the 1989 General Assembly, the Church of the Nazarene added an Article of Faith on the meaning and mission of the Church to the *Manual* (XI, par. 15). This significant statement is a summary of what Nazarenes have long believed themselves to be. The Article of Faith reads:

> We believe in the Church, the community that confesses Jesus Christ as Lord, the covenant people of God made new in Christ, the Body of Christ called together by the Holy Spirit through the Word.
> God calls the Church to express its life in the unity and fellowship of the Spirit; in worship through the preaching of the Word, observance of the sacraments, and ministry in His name; by obedience to Christ and mutual accountability.
> The mission of the Church in the world is to continue the redemptive work of Christ in the power of the Spirit through holy living, evangelism, discipleship, and service.
> The Church is a historical reality, which organizes itself in culturally conditioned forms; exists both as local congregations and as a universal body; sets apart persons called of God for specific ministries. God calls the Church to live under His rule in anticipation of the consummation at the coming of our Lord Jesus Christ.

[Exodus 19:3; Jeremiah 31:33; Matthew 8:11; 10:7; 16:13-19, 24; 18:15-20; 28:19-20; John 17:14-26; 20:21-23; Acts 1:7-8; 2:32-47; 6:1-2; 13:1; 14:23; Romans 2:28-29; 4:16; 10:9-15; 11:13-32; 12:1-8; 15:1-3; 1 Corinthians 3:5-9; 7:17; 11:1, 17-33; 12:3, 12-31; 14:26-40; 2 Corinthians 5:11—6:1; Galatians 5:6, 13-14; 6:1-5, 15; Ephesians 4:1-17; 5:25-27; Philippians 2:1-16; 1 Thessalonians 4:1-12; 1 Timothy 4:13; Hebrews 10:19-25; 1 Peter 1:1-2, 13; 2:4-12, 21; 4:1-2, 10-11; 1 John 4:17; Jude 24; Revelation 5:9-10]

GETTING IT OFF THE PAPER AND INTO LIFE

This all looks good on paper. Now comes the hard part; there is a price to pay in having a healthy body. We need to get this out of the textbook and into the workshop of living. The principles must be incarnated into real live believers who have street addresses and identities. On paper it looks great! We're in the biggest project on earth. But we must "go active." We must begin life application that will enable us to demonstrate our love toward others where we live and serve as Christians.

We do not want you to become lazy, but to imitate those who through faith and patience inherit what has been promised.

HEB. 6:12, NIV

The Disciplines of Your New Life

GORDON WETMORE

Six weeks had passed since Bill found salvation in Christ. The glow of that beautiful experience still lingered, and he loved to talk about it. But tonight he came home tired and perhaps a little down. He was about to learn that to live a life of spiritual victory required some exercise and discipline on his part.

Cindy had dinner ready. Rob, six, and Susan, four, were into the familiar ritual arguing over which TV channel they would watch. Cindy was quieter than usual, and Bill sensed that something was bothering her. After supper he spent a little time with the children and then went to the kitchen to talk to Cindy.

Cindy hesitated to share with Bill what had happened that day. Finally she told him that Joe Smith had called and given some suggestions as to how Bill could improve his efforts as a substitute teacher in the young adult class.

This was Bill's first encounter with criticism from a fellow believer. His thoughts ranged from self-defense to appreciation for Joe's attempt to help him. It led him and Cindy to talk about some broader aspects of Christian growth. For one thing they had both been concerned about developing a more meaningful family altar

GORDON WETMORE is president of Northwest Nazarene College, Nampa, Idaho, and former pastor of First Church, Kansas City.

time both for themselves and for Rob and Susan. Even as a young convert, Bill was becoming aware of his need to be a model as well as a teacher for his children.

The next morning Bill called his pastor and asked if he was available for lunch. Their lunchtime conversation was the beginning of an exciting spiritual adventure for Bill. His understanding of the disciplines of the Christian life took on a new dimension. His questions opened the way for Pastor Williams to deal specifically with spiritual development. They talked about biblical helps for Christian growth as well as the guidelines provided in the *Manual.*

Pastor Williams shared with Bill Col. 2:6-7*a*, "Just as you received Christ Jesus as Lord, continue to live in him, rooted and built up in him" (NIV).

Together they looked at Matt. 5:6-7, "Blessed are those who hunger and thirst for righteousness, for they will be filled. Blessed are the merciful, for they will be shown mercy" (NIV).

The pastor suggested that Bill examine Matthew 25 and note how much emphasis Jesus placed on the discipline of continuing Christian commitment. Then they read together Heb. 6:1, 3, 11-12: "Therefore let us leave the elementary teachings about Christ and go on to maturity. . . . And God permitting, we will do so. . . . We want each of you to show this same diligence to the very end, in order to make your hope sure. We do not want you to become lazy, but to imitate those who through faith and patience inherit what has been promised" (NIV).

Sensing something of Bill's personality and individual needs, Pastor Williams saw that Paul's letters to Timothy would provide a long-term setting for his spiritual discipline and growth. He referred him especially to the passage in 2 Tim. 2:1-7.

Bill was an ardent jogger, and Pastor Williams joined him whenever he could in the physical conditioning. Out of these experiences the young Christian discovered some basic truths about growth. Just as the human body is a gift from God and needs to be developed, so spiritual life requires discipline and conditioning. Together he and the pastor worked out a program for Bill's life that encompassed both Christian discipline and physical development in its three parts: (1) diet, (2) exercise, (3) rest. Diet is the input stage, exercise is the output, and rest is the renewal time. Each stage has several practices.

DIET—INPUT AND INSPIRATION

Quiet Time

This is normally the time set aside for private devotions. The important factors are that it should be personal, regular, and preferably daily. The morning is often the best time, although the specific hour will depend on the individual's schedule. The important thing is to select a time that is devoted to dialogue between a loving Heavenly Father and one's own spirit. The location in which the quiet time takes place is not as important as the personal communion.

Bible Study

Every Christian needs to develop some kind of system that aids him in personal understanding of the Scriptures. Each person should have his or her own Bible. Many find it helpful to mark their Bibles in a way that helps them to remember its contents. Make notes and underline passages in private reading. Also add insights gained from the pastor's sermons and from group Bible studies.

Study the Bible in private devotions. Begin with the Bible itself, not with commentaries or other helps. Frequently the Scriptures, read with a receptive spirit, will speak for themselves as they are illuminated by the Spirit of God. After initial meditation on Scripture itself one may use study aids and thus profit from the research and insightful interpretation of Bible scholars.

Prayer

Prayer is to the spirit what breath is to the body. It is communion with God. A Christian prays to God the Father in the name of Jesus, supported by the power and presence of the Holy Spirit.

Paul tells us the Spirit helps us in our weakness: "We do not know how to pray as we ought, but the Spirit himself intercedes for us" (Rom. 8:26, RSV).

Our praying is a two-way communication. We speak and God listens. He speaks and our hearts respond. The Holy Spirit makes this possible.

We may pray by sharing the concerns of others who likewise are seeking the presence of God. Some beautiful prayers found in the Bible are:

- A prayer for deliverance (Gen. 32:9-12)
- A prayer of dedication (1 Kings 8:22-53)
- An intercessory prayer (Dan. 9:3-19)
- A prayer in time of crisis (Jonah 2:1-9)
- Our Lord's model prayer (Matt. 6:9-13)
- A prayer for Christian growth (Eph. 1:15-19)
- Prayer for a Christ-filled life (Eph. 3:14-19)

Private prayer involves more than making our wants known to God. It is basically a time of communion (communication) with Him. Christian prayer reflects six moods or approaches to God. In mature praying all of them should be included, and usually in the following order: (1) Praise; (2) Thanksgiving; (3) Confession; (4) Intercession; (5) Petition; (6) Adoration.

1. *Praise:* The heart affirms God the Heavenly Father for what and who He is. Praise acknowledges that He is God. Quoting psalms of praise is a helpful way to express our feelings to God.

2. *Thanksgiving:* The Bible suggests that "with thanksgiving let your requests be made known unto God" (Phil. 4:6). The child of God remembers the many blessings for which he is thankful to the Father. Our thanks begin with deep gratitude for salvation, and continue through the great and small blessings of day-by-day life.

3. *Confession:* As God shows us where He wants us to improve, the child of God confesses his shortcomings and failures. So long as we are in this life and are open to Him, God's Holy Spirit will guide us into new truth that makes us more Christlike. So we must keep coming boldly to the throne of grace, confessing our inadequacy and acknowledging our need for His help.

4. *Intercession:* Our greatest ministry as children of God is to bring others to our Heavenly Father in prayer and support. This may well be the longest part of our daily prayers. We talk to God about specific people with known needs. Intercessory prayer completes the network by which God does great things in the lives of those for whom we pray. It also endears them to us and strengthens our agape love.

5. *Petition:* Here, now, we may bring our own concerns to a loving Father. This is no time for bravado or feelings of self-sufficiency. He wants us to be candid; to tell Him our concerns great and small.

6. *Adoration:* Our prayer appropriately ends where it begins in offering praise and adoration to our all-sufficient and eternal Father.

Sensitivity to the Spirit of God

We learn to listen to the voice of the Spirit and to trust Him. As we become more confident of His leadership, we discover more of His guidance, and He shares His burden for the world with us. This partnership with God takes time but it is the stuff from which sturdy saints are made. Such a partnership begins to penetrate all of life. It occurs in the quiet time, in the Bible study, in the place of prayer, and even in times of intense activity.

Self-discipline

Self-discipline involves time management. It calls for establishing priorities for the daily activities so that our lives may be most useful to God. We find our hearts are motivated to order our lives in keeping with His will. We do it with joy and not from compulsion.

Fasting is part of self-discipline. The purpose is to set apart a special time to be with the Father in prayer or to give ourselves to some activity that glorifies His name. Fasting provides time in which our spiritual sensitivities are sharpened and we become more aware of God's direction and purpose.

Jesus tells us that fasting is a covenant between the Heavenly Father and ourselves: "When you fast . . . [conduct yourself] so that it will not be obvious to men that you are fasting, but only to your Father, who is unseen; and your Father, who sees what is done in secret, will reward you" (Matt. 6:17-18, NIV).

Reading and Study

We may enrich our lives and extend our influence by learning from men and women who have walked with God. Many are found in the Bible, but there are others in the life of the church who have also been led of the Spirit. What they have learned, they have shared. We will grow if we discipline ourselves to read each year at least one Christian classic or one current book in which a Christian author shares his walk with God. Some recommended books appear in the appendix.

Nurture by Other Christians

God has given His children brothers and sisters, and He intends that these family members will support each other. He often speaks some of His most practical advice through a fellow Christian who loves us, prays for us, and is there to help in time of our need. A Heavenly Father expects each of us to do the same for brothers and sisters who need an encouraging word or deed.

It is in this mutual ministry and interdependence that Christ comes closest to us. When we give ourselves to a small group of Christians who come to know us, we find that we have a new sense of accountability to them. It is also in these cooperative ministries that God's kingdom moves forward with greatest power.

EXERCISE—OUTPUT AND SERVICE

Worship

Any form of worship is a service to God. Effort and concentration are required. As we follow Christ He asks us to become involved. Jesus makes it plain: "Not everyone who says to me,

'Lord, Lord,' will enter the kingdom of heaven, but only he who does the will of my Father who is in heaven" (Matt. 7:21, NIV).

• *Private worship* can take place in our quiet time or in any other experience where there is reflection on God and His nature. A conscious and disciplined effort is required to thus affirm and adore God.

• *Family worship* is when a household comes together to study the Scriptures, to pray, to sing hymns, and to reflect on God's grace and salvation. It is part of Christian discipline to celebrate family togetherness in times of worship.

Some find early morning the best time; others worship around the dinner table. Still others unite in God's presence in the evening before retiring. Some form of consistent family worship is an integral part of every strong Christian home. (See chapter 9.)

• *Public worship* occurs when God's people gather to offer praise, to unite in prayer, and to listen to the preaching of the Word. At times they celebrate the sacraments. As a service to God, this requires awareness, response, and participation. The Bible admonishes us, "Let us not give up meeting together, as some are in the habit of doing, but let us encourage one another" (Heb. 10:25, NIV).

Scripture Memorization

The Psalmist testified, "I have hidden your word in my heart that I might not sin against you" (Ps. 119:11, NIV). It is wise early in our Christian development to begin a systematic plan of Scripture memorization. Here are some verses that all Christians should have in their memory banks:

Prov. 3:5-6	1 Cor. 10:13
Matt. 6:33	Phil. 4:13
John 3:16	1 John 1:7-9
Rom. 12:1-2	1 John 4:11-12

From the memorization of single verses one can move on to longer passages. Adult Ministries offers a suggested program of helpful Bible memorization in the booklet, *The Word to Live By*. The key is to develop some form of regular memorization.

Discovering God in Daily Life

The real proof of one's devotion to Christ is an obedient life, the avoidance of evil, and the discovery of God's presence in everyday affairs. Paul knew the reality of the divine Presence in the daily round of activities: "Whatever you do, do it all for the glory of God" (1 Cor. 10:31, NIV). He had also found the divine enabling for a difficult task: "I can do all things through Christ which strengtheneth me" (Phil. 4:13). The key to this daily partnership with God is obedience, faithfulness in prayer, Bible study, and the cultivation of the awareness of God's presence.

Stewardship

Christian stewardship begins with the acknowledgment that God owns everything (*Manual*, par. 38). He gave us all that we have. He asks us to manage these resources for Him. He thus works through each of us to bring blessing and aid to His children and to His world. We are partners with God.

A steward is one who stands at the counter of the inexhaustible storehouse of God and dispenses that which is needed for the well-being of His children. The resources are endless because there is no way of exhausting God's supply.

Also involved here is the giving of the tithe to support God's kingdom. Part of the *Manual* statement on "Christian Stewardship" (par. 38) reads as follows:

> God, as a God of system and order in all of His ways, has established a system of giving which acknowledges His ownership and man's stewardship. To this end all His children should faithfully tithe and present offerings for the support of the gospel.

The tithe was instituted in Old Testament times. It is written into the Mosaic law (Lev. 27:30-32), and the prophet Malachi gave a strong statement concerning it when he wrote, "Bring the whole tithe into the storehouse, that there may be food in my house." Then he adds God's promise that if we do, He will "throw open the floodgates of heaven and pour out so much blessing that you will not have room enough for it" (3:10, NIV). Jesus confirmed the tithe as part of the law when He told His hearers, "You should have practiced the latter [tithing], without neglecting the former ['justice, mercy, and faithfulness]" (Matt. 23:23, NIV).

The *Manual* further defines the "storehouse" as the church.

> Storehouse tithing is a scriptural and practical performance of faithfully and regularly placing the tithe into that church to which the member belongs. . . . All who are a part of the Church of the Nazarene are urged to contribute faithfully one-tenth of all their increase as a minimum financial obligation to the Lord and freewill offerings in addition as God has prospered them for the support of the whole church (par. 38.1).

When we pass along God's bounty to others, there is enough for both of us. Paul assures us, "My God will meet all your needs according to his glorious riches in Christ Jesus" (Phil. 4:19, NIV). Consequently, the child of God joyfully gives not only a tithe of his income but also a portion of his time, of his love, and whatever he has to bring blessing to the Church and healing to his world.

Stewardship takes exertion. It is part of the discipline of the Christian life. As we serve others, Christ enriches our own lives and makes us more like himself. For did He not say, "The Son of Man did not come to be served, but to serve" (Matt. 20:28, NIV)?

Servanthood

When the Bible speaks of Jesus as a servant of God it is describing Him in the highest terms. A biblical servant is one who knows very well who his Master is. He knows that his freedom and fulfillment will be the direct result of his faithful service to that Master. It is only such a servant who is truly free. In this spirit the Christian goes about his service to Christ as a responsible citizen both of heaven and of this present world. The servant of God has a divinely bestowed sense of dignity and self-worth. He gives honor where honor is due, but he does not feel obligated to give deference because of human status or rank. He is free to serve the poorest as well as the richest.

God's man realizes that there is no such thing as an independent Christian. Every child of God is under orders to do the work of Christ in the service of the world. The disciplined Christian has learned that he does not have the right to say no when God says go.

Shared Faith

The Body of Christ is a corporate fellowship. It is not made up of isolated individuals. God lays burdens upon other people's hearts for our own needs. At the same time we have a family responsibility for other Christians.

God provides adequate grace when we put forth the needed effort to be faithful and loving laborers in the work of Christ. In this Jesus gives us the honor of being fellow servants with Him in the accomplishment of the Kingdom work. He also tells us that such ministry to others is the evidence of our partnership with Him. "By this shall all men know that ye are my disciples, if ye have love one to another" (John 13:35).

There is not only the sharing of faith within the Christian community but also with those outside. The joy of this life in Christ is too good to keep to ourselves. Every sincere Christian wants to share his faith with others. In fact we are commanded to do so. Some are more gifted than others in personal evangelism, but we all are commissioned to be witnesses. Our testimony by word and by life is a sharing ministry in which every Christian should be involved.

Learning the Will of God

In routine times of life most of our decisions come naturally and easily. When we are faithful in Bible study, prayer, worship, and witness, we find God's will for our lives naturally unfolding.

But even in great, life-changing decisions, God sometimes makes His will so clearly known that we are sure what decision is right. At other times when a difficult or complex decision is called for we must search for the right answer. Often we may find God's answer by following a three-step decision-making process:

1. *A candid sharing* with God every factor that comes to mind that is of consequence in the decision. The point is to let everything come to the surface.

2. *Allow enough time* for the Spirit of God to help us rank these various factors in their order of importance. The key factor is enough time. This may be a few hours or days. Some testify that a week or two is probably enough.

3. *Make the decision.* Here we would like to have God tell us what to do. But He sometimes wants us to exercise God-given and Spirit-guided intelligence. He says to us, "You see what is important and what is not important. Take the most important items and make up your mind on these." He knows that unless we base the decision on what is most important we will never be able to live with it. We must make the decision on this basis, and then never look back.

In this kind of Christian decision-making we rest securely on God's promise, "The steps of a good man are ordered by the Lord" (Ps. 37:23).

REST-RENEWAL AND TRUST

This third part of the cycle of disciplined Christian life is where God's grace brings healing to the stresses and bruises that come with growth and development.

Solitude

Christian solitude is not to be confused with loneliness. It is sometimes identified with the quiet time but it can be achieved even in the midst of strenuous activity. Christian solitude is a shutting out of the traffic of the world and a concentration on the things of the Spirit. The result is an inner serenity and a sense of peace within ourselves, with God, and with our world. This experience reaffirms who we are and what we want to be. Manie Payne Ferguson knew this Christian experience and wrote:

> *Blessed quietness! Holy quietness!*
> *What assurance in my soul!*
> *On the stormy sea Jesus speaks to me,*
> *And the billows cease to roll.*

Meditation

Meditation is a prayerlike attitude that provides for reflection and healing. In times of worship and reflection we may think deeply upon who God is, upon His grace, and His gift of salvation. We are uplifted when we reflect that we are a part of it all. Meditation differs from prayer in that it is not active conversation but a kind of listening or being tuned into God so that He is enabled to give us insight and direction.

Submission

The human spirit will ultimately serve one of two masters. One is Satan; the other is God. We must make the choice. Jesus said, "No man can serve two masters" (Matt. 6:24). It is equally true that everyone serves one. Peace comes only in continuing surrender to a loving Heavenly Father. Out of that submission arises, somewhat to our amazement, a strength and identity that builds character.

Vision

Submitting to God and relaxing in His presence brings the cessation of struggle. From this perspective Christ becomes more a part of our experience. The temporal view blends with the eternal in balance and harmony. The future becomes bright with a sense of purpose and direction.

Discerning Evil

Satan is the clever foe of the Christian. The Bible teaches us that "our struggle is not against flesh and blood, but against the powers of this dark world and against spiritual forces of evil" (Eph. 6:12, NIV). Satan will deceive us if we are not depending on the insight that God's Spirit gives. In this struggle to live a righteous life, however, we are given adequate resources. John advises us, "Test the spirits to see whether they from God" (1 John 4:1, NIV). And in this testing process the Spirit-filled are promised divine assistance. Jesus said of the Holy Spirit, "When he, the Spirit of truth, comes, he will guide you into all truth" (John 16:13, NIV).

Peace and Rest

The covenanted healing touch of God is sensed when we relax our own striving and trust the divine goodness. This rest brings strength and promise. We do not always know just how the details will work out, but we are at ease to leave the extent of the blessing to a loving Father.

At the birth of Jesus the angels sang, "Peace to men on whom his favor rests" (Luke 2:14, NIV). Our Lord reinforces the promise for us in this 20th century. "Peace I leave with you; my peace I give you . . . Do not let your hearts be troubled and do not be afraid" (John 14:27, NIV). God's peace brings ultimate fulfillment to the heart of the disciple.

Andrew Murray gives us a summary for our reflection on Christian disciplines:

> Ordinary Christians imagine all that is not positively forbidden and sinful is lawful to them. They seek to retain as much as possible of this world, with its property, its literature, its enjoyments. The truly consecrated soul, however, is as the soldier who carries only what he needs for the warfare. He lays aside every weight as well as the easily besetting sin. He is afraid of entangling himself too deeply with exclusively earthly affairs. His life is lived as one specially set apart for the Lord and His service.[1]

For one who follows this road, the ancient promise is as current as God's special touch at our morning meditations: "The path of the just is as the shining light, that shineth more and more unto the perfect day" (Prov. 4:18).

He died for all,
that those who live
should no longer live for
themselves but for
him who died
for them.

2 COR. 5:15, NIV

This New Life in the Old World

C. NEIL STRAIT

Jeannette Sanders looked forward with joy to graduation from the Nazarene college where she was completing her senior year. She hoped to teach in the high school near her parents so that she could live at home. They were both in poor health and needed her assistance. The Nazarene church in the community certainly needed her help as well.

She knew that many people had worked hard to improve the quality of education offered in the high school. Jeannette was a mature Christian who had a talent and love for working with students. She had excelled in her college studies and desired to dedicate all of her abilities to her task as a teacher. The educational goals of young people in the small community had been traditionally low, and she hoped to change this.

The school principal had assured Jeannette that she was his choice for the position. But she learned that some school board members were leaning toward another applicant whose training was so poor that to hire her, major exceptions to the professional standards would have to be made. She, too, had been reared in the community but was known as a young woman of question-

C. NEIL STRAIT is superintendent of the Michigan District; formerly pastor, First Church, Lansing, Mich.

able character. She would not provide the kind of responsible teaching and example needed.

Through a woman closely related both to the school board and to Jeannette's family, she learned the story. To obtain the position for herself the poorly trained applicant had offered to pay a substantial sum to a member of the school board. Several committee members made clear their support for Jeannette, but they lacked one vote.

It had been suggested that if she would match the $500 bribe offered the corrupt board member she could be hired and her purpose for wanting to teach in the community could be fulfilled. But if she refused to cooperate, the incompetent teacher would have the position, the students' education would suffer, her parents would be without her help, and the church would be without a Sunday School teacher.

What should she do? She wants her decisions to be shaped by the Spirit of Christ, by the teachings of the Bible and the guidance of her church. But she must weigh the values and make the decision.

*   *   *

What was different about Jeannette? Why was her problem bigger than raising $500 to sway the election?

The "new life in Christ" experience ushers one into the arena of decision making. For, having been converted—changed from the old self to a "new creation"—the basis for action has changed. Before conversion one acted only out of self-interest. But now, self has been brought under the authority of Christ and the approach is different.

Paul reminds us: "He died for all, that those who live should no longer live for themselves but for him who died for them" (2 Cor. 5:15, NIV).

POWER TO CHOOSE

The Christian does not at the moment of conversion forfeit his freedom to choose. Indeed, it is his in a greater capacity. "In

Christ" he has the freedom to choose what he *ought,* not just what
he *wants.*

The *Manual of the Church of the Nazarene* states this about
free agency: "We believe that man's creation in Godlikeness included ability to choose between right and wrong, and that thus
he was made morally responsible" (*Manual,* par. 7).

Decision Making and Consequences

Jeannette does not have to ask twice what it is she wants—
she wants the job! Her pre-Christian choice would have been to
pay the $500, get the job, and forget about it. The decision would
have been rationalized by the axiom, "Everybody's doing it." Jeannette's life-style before conversion would have been to go the
"situation-ethics" route. This means using the rationale that whatever is convenient is right. Such choosing would take life onward
but not upward.

But another factor needs to be considered. E. Stanley Jones
has said that, "We are free to choose, but we are not free to choose
the consequences of our choosing." The difference between the
sinner and the Christian is that the Christian cares about the consequences of his choices, while the sinner believes he can ignore
them and beat the odds.

William Barclay and others have adequately reminded us
that we cannot "break" the Commandments—we only break ourselves. In decision making, we need to know that choices are important, for they are the material out of which character is made.
Paul says: "Were you not raised to life with Christ? Then aspire to
the realm above, where Christ is, seated at the right hand of God,
and let your thoughts dwell on that higher realm, not on this
earthly life" (Col. 3:1-2, NEB).

Ethics—Doing the Truth

Decision making involves ethics. Someone has described
ethics as "doing the truth." The Christian looks for ways to do the
truth and recognizes that behind each choice there are factors beyond self and beyond the moment.

Ethics becomes that broader interpretation of how we live
out—express in the world—our faith, our values, our principles.

The hardest "growth steps" for the new Christian are those wherein he must change the cadence of his life. Because of conversion he is now "marching to a new drummer." And the growing process involves "getting in step" with the Word, with the right, and with Christ. The Christ-follower is one who is making constant adjustments in his life—adjustment to the Word, to the right, and to the values that are forming in the converted life.

Commitment to Lordship

The basic foundation for Christian choice must be a commitment to Jesus as Lord of life. The "new creation" that takes place in conversion brings a spiritual authority to the center of life, Jesus Christ. When life orders its choices, its priorities, and its ways according to this authority, then choices are made that will bring glory to that Lordship.

Commitment means that through conversion life has come under a new leader, a new authority. It means that life has pledged itself, its choices, and its ethics to a new Commander-in-chief. The decisions have been entrusted to Christ and the consequences for such decisions are in His custody.

Jeannette, whose decision-making dilemma we related at the beginning of this chapter, must rest her decision on the side of right, knowing that, while it may hurt for the moment, it is the best in the long run. For, to place our choices in the custody of Jesus Christ is to be committed to such trust and to believe that He wills our best, even when the choices are hard. If we do the right things and leave the results with God, then the right results will follow.

THE COMMANDMENTS ARE WRITTEN INTO LIFE

God's commandments are written into life. They are registered in creation. All that God has created has the mark of His truth and ways. And man is a perfect example of this. Genesis chapters 2 and 3 tell us about God's first commandment and man's first moral choice. When life is lived in obedience to the ways of God there is peace in the inner man and fulfillment in his life. All of that is disturbed when man violates the commands and transgresses the ways of God. And this is because the laws of God, and the consequences to them, are written into the fabric of life.

The new Christian faces decisions involving right and wrong. Early in his walk with Christ he asks, "How, then, should I live?" It is at this point that the church offers help through ethical guidance of the general and special rules. In the *Manual* section, "The Christian Life," there are these statements:

> The church joyfully proclaims the good news that we may be delivered from all sin to a new life in Christ. By the grace of God we Christians are to "put off the old"—the old patterns of conduct as well as the old carnal mind—and are to "put on the new"—a new and holy way of life as well as the mind of Christ (Ephesians 4:17-24).
>
> The Church of the Nazarene purposes to relate timeless biblical principles to contemporary society in such a way that the doctrines and rules of the church may be known and understood in many lands and within a variety of cultures. We hold that the Ten Commandments, as reaffirmed in the New Testament, constitute the basic Christian ethic and ought to be obeyed in all particulars (*Manual,* pars. 33, 33.1)

Individual Conscience

A key influence over our decisions is conscience. And what is it? Conscience is that voice or guidance that enlightens our hearts and minds in regard to life's choices and opportunities.

We need to understand that because of sin the conscience of the unconverted is not always a reliable guide. Someone has said that it often sends out distorted signals. Sin shuts out the light of the Word. Sin invites life to rationalize and seek the self way. Sin opposes right and reinforces wrong. And when sin has dominated one's life, conscience may be seared until it does not speak loudly and clearly about wrongdoing. After one has been born again, the Holy Spirit will begin to awaken his conscience and it will provide proper guidance for his choices.

Conscience of the Church

We recognize that the church is a community of faith—a community of believers, under God. The strength of such community lies in acknowledging that no man is an island and that each person draws support and strength from others.

In our ethical rules we have the collective conscience of the church, influenced and guided by the Holy Spirit. Godly people have recorded their conclusions about holy living. The new Christian is encouraged to allow the conscience of the church to be his "schoolmaster" (to use the apostle Paul's term) in determining his values and in educating his conscience. The *Manual* states:

> It is further recognized that there is validity in the concept of the collective Christian conscience as illuminated and guided by the Holy Spirit. The Church of the Nazarene, as an international expression of the Body of Christ, acknowledges its responsibility to seek ways to particularize the Christian life so as to lead to a holiness ethic. The historic ethical standards of the church are expressed in part in the following items. They should be followed carefully and conscientiously as guides and helps to holy living. Those who violate the conscience of the church do so at their own peril and to the hurt of the witness of the Church (*Manual*, par. 33.2).

We recognize in society the right of any voluntary organization to set forth its values, principles, guidelines, and so forth. In this way, those who become a part of the organization know clearly what it is about. The same principle applies to the church. The counsel of God-ordained leaders who speak through the voice of the General Assembly should be carefully considered. Heb. 13:17 advises, "Obey your leaders and submit to their authority. They keep watch over you as men who must give an account" (NIV).

GENERAL AND SPECIAL RULES

The church sets forth its major ethical principles through its general and special rules. These rules are Bible-based and reflect timeless principles that have been in the mainstream of the Christian faith from the beginning. Their importance to Christian development is to be taken seriously.

Doing Good

In developing the new life-style of the Christian, it is imperative that we see the true intent of these rules. It is to lift living to the quality of life that the church deems important for developing the spiritual potential of the believer.

The *Manual* states:

> They [members of the Body of Christ] shall evidence their commitment to God—
>
> FIRST. By doing that which is enjoined in the Word of God, which is our rule of both faith and practice, including:
>
> (1) Loving God with all the heart, soul, mind, and strength, and one's neighbor as oneself [Exodus 20:3-6; Leviticus 19:17-18; Deuteronomy 5:7-10; 6:4-5; Mark 12:28-31; Romans 13:8-10] (pars. 27, 27.1).

The decision-making process, for the new Christian, involves choices not only between right and wrong but between the better and the best. The general rules invite us to positive steps of fulfilling the love of God and our love to our fellowmen.

Al Truesdale has stated that Jesus reaffirmed the authority of God's ethical requirements in two ways: (1) He showed that love is basic. If we truly love God we will obey Him; if we honestly love people we will seek their good and do them no injury. Therefore He says, " 'Love the Lord your God with all your heart . . . [and] Love your neighbor as yourself.' All the Law and the Prophets hang on these two commandments" (Matt. 22:37, 39-40, NIV). (2) But Jesus knew also that universal principles need to be spelled out in specific instructions.

Other general rules help us see the positive witness to our love for Christ. They are:

> (2) Pressing upon the attention of the unsaved the claims of the gospel, inviting them to the house of the Lord, and trying to compass their salvation [Matthew 28:19-20; Acts 1:8; Romans 1:14-16; 2 Corinthians 5:18-20].
>
> (3) Being courteous to all men [Ephesians 4:32; Titus 3:2; 1 Peter 2:17; 1 John 3:18].
>
> (4) Being helpful to those who are also of the faith, in love

forbearing one another [Romans 12:13; Galatians 6:2, 10; Colossians 3:12-14].

(5) Seeking to do good to the bodies and souls of men; feeding the hungry, clothing the naked, visiting the sick and imprisoned, and ministering to the needy, as opportunity and ability are given [Matthew 25:35-36; 2 Corinthians 9:8-10; Galatians 2:10; James 2:15-16; 1 John 3:17-18] (*Manual*, par. 27.1).

These are all positive expressions of our love. Where these are practiced consistently, the focus of life is positive and fulfilling.

Avoiding Evil

The next section of the general rules deals with "avoiding evil of every kind." These, too, are based on biblical principles.

(1) Taking the name of God in vain [Exodus 20:7; Leviticus 19:12; James 5:12].

(2) Profaning of the Lord's Day by participation in unnecessary secular activities, thereby indulging in practices which deny its sanctity [Exodus 20:8-11; Isaiah 58:13-14; Mark 2:27-28; Acts 20:7; Revelation 1:10].

(3) Sexual immorality, such as premarital or extra marital relations, perversion in any form, or looseness and impropriety of conduct [Exodus 20:14; Matthew 5:27-32; 1 Corinthians 6:9-11; Galatians 5:19; 1 Thessalonians 4:3-7].

(4) Habits or practices known to be destructive of physical and mental well-being. Christians are to regard themselves as temples of the Holy Spirit [Proverbs 20:1; 23:1-3; 1 Corinthians 6:17-20; 2 Corinthians 7:1; Ephesians 5:18].

(5) Quarreling, returning evil for evil, gossiping, slandering, spreading surmises injurious to the good names of others [2 Corinthians 12:20; Galatians 5:15; Ephesians 4:30-32; James 3:5-18; 1 Peter 3:9-10].

(6) Dishonesty, taking advantage in buying and selling, bearing false witness, and like works of darkness [Leviticus 19:10-11; Romans 12:17; 1 Corinthians 6:7-10].

(7) The indulging of pride in dress or behavior. Our people are to dress with the Christian simplicity and modesty that become holiness [Proverbs 29:23; 1 Timothy 2:8-10; James 4:6; 1 Peter 3:3-4; 1 John 2:15-17].

(8) Music, literature, and entertainments that dishonor God [1 Corinthians 10:31; 2 Corinthians 6:14-17; James 4:4] (*Manual*, par. 27.2).

Special Rules

Contained in the *Manual* are also special rules that amplify the General Rules and express the church's combining judgment on several social concerns. Some of these are:

MARRIAGE AND DIVORCE
(*Manual*, par. 35)

ABORTION
(*Manual*, par. 36)

HUMAN SEXUALITY
(*Manual*, par. 37)

CHRISTIAN STEWARDSHIP
(*Manual*, par. 38)

GUIDING PRINCIPLES

You will want to discuss all of these special rules with your pastor and let him explain the Bible-based reasons for them. But by way of illustration, let's look at some of the broad principles that make them logical.

Mastered by Christ

The Christian has one Master—the Lord Jesus Christ. One of the strongest arguments for total abstinence from alcoholic beverages, tobacco, and narcotics (*Manual*, pars. 34.5 and 34.6) is that a disciple will not give the mastery of his life to anyone or anything but the Savior. Multiplied millions of people are hopelessly bound by these destructive habits. Listen to the apostle Paul's testimony: "I may do anything I please, but not everything I may do is good for me. I may do anything I please; but I am not going to let anything master me" (1 Cor. 6:12, Goodspeed).

God's power can free one from the bondage of such habit patterns and enable him to give the total mastery of his life to the Lord.

Influence

Another scriptural guideline for Christian conduct is "How will this activity affect my influence for Christ?" Read the eighth chapter of First Corinthians. It contains timeless truth concerning one's witness to other Christians.

Then the *Manual* suggests that we have an obligation to witness against such social evils as violence, sensuality, pornography, profanity, and the occult, as portrayed by and through the commercial entertainment industry in its many forms and to endeavor to bring about the demise of enterprises known to be the purveyors of this kind of entertainment.

General Superintendent George Coulter called this "the protest of our prohibitions." It is sanctified good sense to compeltely boycott forms of entertainment that are diametrically opposed to Christian morality and holy living.

Spiritual Sensitivity

God's children have more than human help in making decisions about ethical choices. Listen to *Manual,* par. 33.3:

> In listing practices to be avoided we recoguize that no catalog, however inclusive, can hope to encompass all forms of evil throughout the world. Therefore it is imperative that our people earnestly seek the aid of the Spirit in cultivating a sensitivity to evil which transcends the mere letter of the law; remembering the admonition: "Prove all things; hold fast that which is good. Abstain from all appearance of evil" (1 Thessalonians 5:21-22).

The Holy Spirit will guide the sincere disciple as he opens his mind and heart to divine direction.

New Values

New life in Christ includes a whole new set of values and convictions. Because she is a Christian, Jeannette will make her decision on the basis of her new value system.

Values are principles, standards, or qualities that we consider worthwhile. They are developed through careful study of God's Word and openness to the instruction of God's Spirit. These basic values will motivate our choices.

Real convictions are built on the foundation of God-given values. They are Bible-based. Charles Allen declared that "a conviction is something that makes one a convict."[1] That's strong language! He goes on, "It chains . . . binds . . . and imprisons. . . . When you are gripped by a belief you are not free anymore. Your belief becomes the controlling force of your life."

The disciple is a convict of Christ. It is "love slavery." No standard is too high. No demand is too costly.

CHRISTLIKE CONDUCT

These ethical principles, biblical guidelines, and personal convictions are more than checks on a spiritual grading scale. Living by these rules must produce more than just a badge of piety. The highest standard is Christlikeness—"For to me to live is Christ" (Phil. 1:21). The final growth goal to be attained by making correct moral choices is that we may come to "the measure of the stature of the fulness of Christ" (Eph. 4:13*b*).

Jeannette's choice finally narrowed down to the question, "What would Jesus do?" That is the final question in every ethical choice a Christian makes. *In His Steps,* by Charles M. Sheldon, tells the fictional story of a church that was dynamically transformed when its members began to ask themselves, "What would Jesus do?" But that is more fact than fiction. Not just churches but homes and businesses and whole communities will feel the impact of such Christlike conduct.

Christian disciple, dare to be different. "Let your light so shine before men, that they may see your good works, and glorify your Father [who] is in heaven" (Matt. 5:16). Then your new life in Christ will make all the difference in this old world.

*These commandments
that I give you today
are to be
upon your hearts.
Impress them
on your children.
Talk about them
when you sit at home.*

DEUT. 6:6-7, NIV

Discipleship Begins at Home

JERRY D. LAMBERT

Eric Swanson was determined to make himself indispensable to International Investments Corporation. He wanted to be sure they couldn't do without him—even if it meant unlimited hours away from his family.

The efforts of this young father were paying off in frequent promotions and salary increases. Eric felt justified in his total commitment to his job. But then a senior officer left the company after many years of service. Eric noted that the man left behind him little impact on the lives of his associates in spite of his hard work. It made him reevaluate his own life and goals. What difference would his life make if he gave everything he had to his work? More money perhaps, or higher position. But would these compensate for the sense of isolation from his wife and children that he was already feeling? He had some misgivings about it.

THE FOUNDATION OF A HAPPY HOME

Some homes are like sand dunes, formed by outside influences instead of by the goals and purposes of its members.

JERRY D. LAMBERT is president of Nazarene Bible College, Colorado Springs, and former superintendent of the Pittsburgh District.

Christian Marriage

Paul said, "Let every man take heed how he buildeth" (1 Cor. 3:10). The time to consider the future of a family is before marriage. It is God's design that believers should marry believers. To attempt marriage with the thought of evangelizing the unsaved mate is both dangerous and unscriptural. It is like building a house upon shifting sands. The church offers helpful resources to the couple contemplating marriage.

> Ministers of the Church of the Nazarene . . . shall seek, in every manner possible, to convey to their congregations the sacredness of Christian marriage. They shall provide premarital counseling in every instance possible before performing a marriage ceremony. They shall only solemnize marriages of persons having the scriptural right to marry (*Manual,* par. 35.1).

The Church, as the Body of Christ, teacher and discipler of God's family, must speak to the issue of Christian marriages. The Church of the Nazarene offers guidance for parents and pastors in presenting the Christian view of marriage to our young people. We read in the *Manual:*

> The Christian family, knit together in a common bond through Jesus Christ, is a circle of love, fellowship, and worship to be earnestly cultivated in a society in which family ties are easily dissolved. We urge upon the ministry and congregations of our church such teachings and practices as will strengthen and develop family ties.
>
> The institution of marriage was ordained of God in the time of man's innocence, and is, according to apostolic authority, "honourable in all"; it is the mutual union of one man and one woman for fellowship, helpfulness, and the propagation of the race. Our people should cherish this sacred estate as becomes Christians, and should enter it only after earnest prayer for divine direction, and when assured that the contemplated union is in accordance with scriptural requirements. They should seek earnestly the blessings which God has ordained in connection with the wedded state, namely, holy companionship, parenthood, and mutual love—the elements of home building. The marriage covenant is morally binding so long as both shall live, and therefore, may not be dissolved at will (par. 35).

It is possible to have a "family built in a common bond through Jesus Christ as a circle of love, fellowship and worship," but only when we follow the scriptural admonition, "Do not be yoked together with unbelievers" (2 Cor. 6:14, NIV). When Moses went a second time up Mount Sinai to receive the Law written on tablets of stone, he was given a command from God to separate the children of Israel from their unbelieving neighbors. God said, "Nor must thou find wives for thy sons among their daughters. Faithless themselves, they will make thy sons, too, faithless and worshippers of their own gods" (see Exod. 34:15-16).

The Single Home

A significant cultural development in our day is the increasing number of those who are choosing to remain single—both men and women. They, too, are establishing homes but in a different framework from that of the family. The motivation for such a choice varies significantly. There may be selfish reasons for remaining single, but sincere Christians do not view the choice that way. Rather they find in singleness greater freedom and opportunity to serve others. Their energies are channeled into the larger family of the church where they are making significant contributions. Even their homes are centers of spiritual activity in no less measure than family-oriented ones.

The Influence of a Christian Home

What difference can one family make? Adam and Eve built a family—or did they? That family rebelled against the commands of God, resulting in a family murder and a fallen race. By contrast, Noah and his family obeyed God, and not only received a fresh start for themselves, but for the succeeding generations as well. Abraham, who lamented he had no child of his own, was given a promise from God. Through his son Isaac, a nation would grow up whom God would bless with the plan of salvation for all mankind. Also, from another family, the household of David, came Mary and Joseph. They were chosen to raise the only begotten Son of God, our Savior and Lord.

It is possible that Adam and Eve did not consider the ultimate consequences of their decision to disobey God and to live their own lives. God's warning, "Ye shall surely die," might have been more bearable if it had meant instant physical death instead of instant spiritual separation from God and future physical death. Death might have been preferable to living outside the Garden of Eden in a broken relationship with God and with the tragic loss of two sons.

A home begins with two people who have thought beyond themselves and beyond the life-style they might choose for themselves. A home begins when two people have committed themselves to a life of submission to each other. As long as they live, their lives will be tightly woven together into the oneness of which the Bible speaks (Gen. 2:24). This relationship must always be surrendered to the Lordship of Christ. Being His disciple will influence and improve the relationship between husband and wife to their golden wedding anniversary and beyond.

Parenting is one of God's special gifts and it is a demanding responsibility. Our faith moves across generations for these concerns by parents carry over into their relationships with their sons and daughters and their spouses and flows on to their grandchildren.

Dietrich Bonhoeffer was thrown into prison during the Nazi control of Germany because he dared to speak out against Hitler and his policies. From his prison cell, deprived of normal human relationships, he was able to focus his heart and mind more clearly upon the meaning of love and marriage. When asked to prepare a marriage ceremony for his niece's wedding, he wrote:

> Marriage is more than your love for each other. It has a higher dignity and power, for it is God's holy ordinance, through which He wills to perpetuate the human race till the end of time. In your love you see only your two selves in the world, but in marriage you are a link in the chain of the generations, which God causes to come and to pass away to His glory, and calls into His kingdom. In your love you see only the heaven of your happiness, but in marriage you are placed at a post of responsibility towards the world and mankind. Your love is your own private possession, but marriage is more than something personal—it is a status, an office.[1]

The following statements present some ideal qualities of a Christian marriage and home. Do your feelings and goals ring true with these?

WHAT IS A CHRISTIAN HOME?

- A Christian home is a place where a family can live in a balanced environment created by God's presence for the growth and nurture of God's people.

- It is the laboratory of human relationships that is best equipped for testing and developing Christian faith in an atmosphere of love and acceptance.

- Home is a place where parents help their children discover they are made in the image of God, redeemable and with a worthwhile purpose.

- It is where people are bound together in lifelong relationships that are used by God to shape and mold them.

- A Christian home is a shelter in the time of trouble. When one member hurts, the others care and minister with healing love.

- It is a place where truth is lived and taught as in no other place on earth.

Shaping Our Children

A recent study quizzed Christian young people to determine who had the greatest influence on their lives. It was a little surprising that the highest percentage of the young people felt their parents were number one. The most unexpected reaction, however, was that "significant other adults" were second in importance, and their teen friends were third. These conclusions present strong implications for the future of both home and church.

Home and Church Share Common Goals

Lyle Jacobson writes, "God has designed the church and family to work together in the development of youth. We know this is true because God has given both institutions several common characteristics."[2]

Most would agree that the home and church share joint responsibility in the spiritual nurture of a child. Parents who leave it entirely to the church will be disappointed in the finished product, for what can be expected from only three to five hours of church-related activities a week? Church leaders are crippled without quality time and support from parents in the spiritual development of children in the Christian home.

Parents Disciple Children

The answer to this question was so basic in the Jewish religion that it was written on bracelets and headbands fastened to their bodies. These served as constant reminders of the commands of God.

> These are the commands, decrees and laws the LORD your God directed me to teach you to observe . . . so that you, your children and their children after them . . . may enjoy long life (*Deut.* 6:1-2, *NIV*).
>
> Hear, O Israel: The LORD our God, the LORD is one. Love the LORD your God with all your heart and with all your soul and with all your strength. These commandments that I give you today are to be upon your hearts. Impress them on your children. Talk about them when you sit at home and when you walk along the road, when you lie down and when you get up. Tie them as symbols on your hands and bind them on your foreheads. Write them on the doorframes of your houses and on your gates (*Deut.* 6:4-9, *NIV*).

According to the scripture, discipling in the home takes place when parents lead their children into a love-relationship with the Lord, then follow through by teaching the life-style that pleases God and enables the young believer to follow God. To be effective, discipling must be done by precept and by example, formally and informally, planned and unplanned, around the house and out for a walk, early in the morning and late at night. God's love and truth must be indelibly written upon the hearts of our children.

The Family Altar: Old but Good

Under difficult circumstances, Father Abraham modeled discipleship for future generations. He was a nomadic shepherd who often moved his flocks and family to find water and green pastures. Abraham, however, made it a top priority to build an altar to the Lord as soon as they arrived at a new location. Disciple-making involves family worship of some kind on a daily basis. It provides an informal time of Scripture study and prayer not possible in a regular church setting and thus undergirds and supports the Sunday worship with God's larger family. Many children learn first to pray with Mom or Dad leading them. Many ask Jesus into their hearts at a family altar time.

How Parents Teach

The spiritual life is a journey. It begins with conversion and continues throughout the Christian life, as believers are molded into Christ's image. The Christian way of life is best taught and modeled in the home.

Because people all around believe and live so differently from the Christian life-style, childhood and youth are frightening and confusing times. What Mom and Dad believe and live are stabilizing forces when a young person is caught in a time of difficult decision. Long before they think to ask, "What would Jesus do?" kids ask themselves, "What would Mom do? How would Dad react?" They have a right to know what we believe. Hopefully they can see it in how we live.

Church Membership Begins at Home

One of the greatest joys Christian parents can know is when a child accepts Christ, desires to be baptized, and joins the church. Pastor's classes are important, but they are most successful in influencing youth when they confirm and reinforce teaching and example that has already taken place in the home. Issues of right and wrong should not be relegated to public school or left entirely to the Sunday School. Early in the lives of our children, we need to begin sharing the specifics of a Christian life-style. These are outlined for us in the general and special rules of the church (*Manual*, pars. 27, 33-38). As a family, we believe this life-style is what God expects of us.

A good family project would be to study together these patterns for Christian living. They are scripturally sound. We can be proud of our heritage, which deals openly with the moral and ethical implications involved in living out the Christian life.

DISCIPLING AND PARENTING

In the letter to the Ephesians we find biblical foundations for the Christian home. The husband and father is to be an active participant as spiritual leader. To all Christians, husbands and wives alike, Paul writes:

> Be imitators of God, therefore, as dearly loved children and live a life of love, just as Christ loved us and gave himself up for us as a fragrant offering and sacrifice to God *(5:1, NIV)*.

> Be careful, then, how you live—not as unwise but as wise, making the most of every opportunity, because the days are evil. Therefore, do not be foolish but understand what the Lord's will is *(5:15-17, NIV)*.

> Submit to one another out of reverence for Christ. Wives, submit to your husbands as to the Lord. For the husband is the head of the wife as Christ is the head of the church, his body, of which he is the Savior. Now as the church submits to Christ, so also wives should submit to their husbands in everything. Husbands, love your wives, just as Christ loved the church. . . . In this same way, husbands ought to love their wives as their own bodies. He who loves his wife loves himself . . . "For this reason a man will leave his father and mother and be united to his wife, and the two will become one flesh" *(5:21-25, 28, 31, NIV)*.

> Children, obey your parents in the Lord, for this is right. "Honor your father and mother"—which is the first commandment with a promise—that it may go well with you and that you may enjoy long life on the earth." Fathers, do not exasperate your children; instead, bring them up in the training and instruction of the Lord *(6:1-4, NIV)*.

Diagrammed, the truth of this Scripture looks like this:

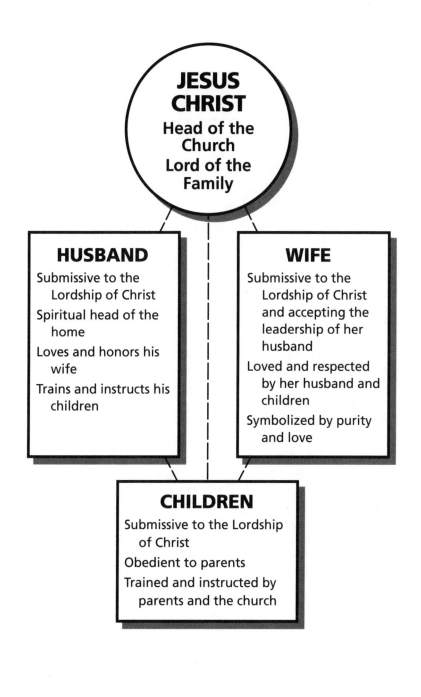

JESUS CHRIST

Head of the Church
Lord of the Family

HUSBAND

Submissive to the Lordship of Christ

Spiritual head of the home

Loves and honors his wife

Trains and instructs his children

WIFE

Submissive to the Lordship of Christ and accepting the leadership of her husband

Loved and respected by her husband and children

Symbolized by purity and love

CHILDREN

Submissive to the Lordship of Christ

Obedient to parents

Trained and instructed by parents and the church

Fathering Is Important

Fathers—even Christian fathers—sometimes believe their only responsibility is "to bring home the bacon" and that mother's job is to take care of the home and raise the children. This idea is not adequate in rearing Christian families because it is contrary to the Scriptures.

It is possible for fathers to accept intellectually their spiritual leadership role in the home without really making it work. They never become the spiritual head of the home. After the children arrive, they hurry away to other interests and involvements in their own lives. Some spend their lives selfishly building their own kingdoms even when it means ignoring or at least neglecting the needs of wife and children.

Christian fathers are to be "imitators of God . . . liv[ing] a life of love . . . not as unwise but as wise, making the most of every opportunity . . . not . . . foolish but understanding what the Lord's will is" (Eph. 5:1*a*, 2*a*, 15*b*-16*a*, 17, NIV). According to the Scriptures, it is the father's responsibility to nurture his children and to bring them up in the training and instruction of the Lord.

In the Old Testament, the family was not only a social unit, but also a spiritual community with religious feasts and holy days to be observed. The earthly father served as a priest, with all of the family taking part in sacrifice and worship.

In New Testament times, God used the home in which Jesus was born to nurture and prepare His Son for His divine mission. The word *husband* originally meant the "house-band" that held the home together. In New Testament evangelism when the husband was converted to Christ, often his household came with him. Entire families were baptized into the Christian faith because they already had learned to follow the spiritual leadership of the father.

Mothering Cannot Be Replaced

When God was planning the birth of Jesus, He chose Mary to mother and nurture His Son. We know very little about the life of Joseph, but we know a great deal about Mary. Her impact upon Jesus is revealed in many ways through His earthly ministry. Her love and loyalty to Him are seen most clearly as she stood at His feet during the Crucifixion.

The apostle Paul was a tremendous influence upon Timothy, but Paul tells us it was Eunice and Lois, Timothy's mother and grandmother, who most positively impacted his life. Paul wrote to Timothy, "Continue in what you have learned and have become convinced of, because you know those from whom you learned it, and how from infancy you have known the holy Scriptures, which are able to make you wise for salvation through faith in Christ Jesus" (2 Tim. 3:14-15, NIV).

Many voices call to women today. Other interests vie for their time and attention. But nothing is as necessary or challenging as the role of mothering; nothing can take its place in the life of a child.

An Associated Press headline read: "Lack of Love Blamed for Infants' Woes." Said the reporter:

> There's not a wonder drug in the world that will cure some of the languishing infants brought to St. Christopher's Hospital for Children. Each month three or four tiny patients are admitted for "failure to thrive." Doctors believe the infants are suffering physically from a lack of love. The babies' symptoms include severe diarrhea and dehydration. They are smaller and lighter than the average tot and some of them scream to be held.

Suzanna Wesley, mother of 19 children, must have felt pressure to do other things. But she took time every day to spend significant moments with each of her children. Through her godly influence on her sons, John and Charles, she played an important part in the 19th-century revival of England, the founding of the Methodist church, and indirectly in the origin of the Church of the Nazarene.

Erosion of an Ideal

Perhaps the greatest hindrance to the family today is the erosion of the high ideal that a happy home is a live option. Magazines, newspapers, and many books question whether the home, as we know it now, can survive in the last years of the 20th century. Millions of children live in broken homes.

The church is struggling in the midst of these changes to minister to people involved in home crises. Since many of these homes are missing a father, it is important that families, especially Christian men, find ways of reaching out to children who are without a dad. Many churches involve men as teachers and group leaders with all ages of children. Caravan, Scouts, and Sunday School classes offer opportunities for children to relate to Christian men who understand fathering.

The church is responsible to God to take positive steps to strengthen the ideal of the home, especially in the hearts of the young. Helpless as we may feel to change all of society, we do have opportunities to guide the people to whom we minister toward a Christian view of marriage and the home.

In the light of scriptural teaching, it is distressing that more and more believers seem to feel that divorce is an acceptable option to escape problems in the home. The counsel of the church is clear to her members who contemplate divorce:

> Members of the Church of the Nazarene are to seek prayerfully a redemptive course of action when involved in marital unhappiness, in full harmony with their vows and the clear teachings of the Scripture, their aim being to save the home and safeguard the good name of both Christ and His Church. Couples having serious marital problems are urged to seek counsel and guidance of their pastor. Failure to comply with this procedure in good faith and with sincere endeavor to seek a Christian solution, and subsequent obtainment of an unscriptural divorce and remarriage, makes one or both parties subject to discipline (par. 35.2).

The church seeks to be redemptive. Its goal is to prevent the tragedy of divorce. But to those who have suffered the pain of such an experience, the church reaches out its hand. We say to them:

> Through ignorance, sin, and human frailties, many in our society fall short of the divine ideal. We believe that Christ can redeem these persons even as He did the woman at Samaria's well. Where the scriptural ground for divorce did not exist and remarriage followed, the marriage partners, upon genuine repentance for their sin, are enjoined to seek the forgiving grace of God and His redemptive help in their marriage relation. Such persons may be received into the membership of the church at such time as they have given evidence of their regeneration and an awareness of their understanding of the sanctity of Christian marriage (par. 35.4).

The Goal of the Christian Home

If the apostle Paul were speaking to families in the midst of 20th-century turmoil, he would probably say again what he said to the family of God in the 1st century:

> I urge you to live a life worthy of the calling you have received. Be completely humble and gentle; be patient, bearing with one another in love. Make every effort to keep the unity of the Spirit through the bond of peace *(Eph. 4:1-3, NIV).*

*   *   *

The Eric Swansons need to learn that homes are not built "on the side." They demand prime time. To endure, they need sound foundations and substantial structural components carefully put together. The necessary foundation is Christian faith and mutual understanding. The structure consists of love, concern, sharing, and ministry to one another, put together piece by piece over the years. It is a joint project involving both parents and children in a caring fellowship.

Not always will the parts dovetail perfectly, but given a willingness to adjust and a desire to find solutions, a noble and enduring structure can be built. God wills it so and the church stands ready to help make it possible.

*In his great mercy
he has given us new
birth into a living
hope through the
resurrection of Jesus
Christ from the dead.*

1 PET. 1:3, NIV

Your New Life
in Christ
Produces Hope

MILLARD REED

Their eyes, red from much weeping, revealed that overpowering stress experienced by parents who have spent anxious hours outside an intensive care room in a hospital where a child was struggling for life. Six days of thorough examination had confirmed their suspicions of the worst kind. A frantic trip halfway across the state had finally brought Fred and Mary to the big University Hospital.

Now after another 24 hours of waiting and weeping they had been given the verdict of the doctors: "Your six-year-old Danny has terminal cancer. Treatment may extend his life briefly, but it would be very painful for him. You must decide soon if you want us to begin the therapy. We'll wait for your decision."

Fred and Mary were the solid, pillar-of-the-church type of Christians. They had been active in the church for years and had been an encouragement to many others in hours of stress and grief. But now they were the sufferers.

The distraught mother cried, "I cannot accept either option. I cannot let my Danny be hurt if it won't really help him. On the other hand, I cannot stand by and do nothing."

MILLARD REED is president of Trevecca Nazarene College and former pastor of Nashville First Church.

"Pastor Reed," asked Fred, "is there any guidance for us? Is there any answer in the Scripture? What can we do in such a hopeless situation?"

The details are unique, but the scene is familiar. Hundreds of pastors have gone with thousands of their people through the same valley of hopelessness and have made sincere but feeble efforts to offer some ray of light in the darkness. Even now, I reached out from my heart to Fred and Mary. I wept with them. We leaned heavily on one another. But my mind was fumbling.

I thought of the scripture, "Let not your heart be troubled" (John 14:1). But it seemed small comfort.

I thought of promises such as: "If ye abide in me, and my words abide in you, ye shall ask what ye will, and it shall be done unto you" (John 15:7). But it did not seem the proper time to quote them.

I thought of the Articles of Faith that declare our confidence in divine healing (XIV), the resurrection (XVI), and the Second Coming (XV). But none of these statements could force their way to my tongue as I shared the anguish of their overwhelming sense of hopelessness.

The Scriptures are sure, the promises are true, and the Articles of Faith are sound. Yet in our actual moment of despair that precious couple and I could not translate their deep meanings into the painful situation in which we were engulfed. It is hard to understand, but sometimes God's greatest truths can get lost in the process of our trying to apply them to traumatic problems. He provides them for our edification. They are disclosures of His very nature. They may be exactly what our souls hunger for and need at a particular time, but the stress that accompanies our hour of grief distorts our understanding and makes it impossible for us to see God's provision for us. We can't seem to apply the balm of that truth to our aching hearts. For a time we suffer on.

Eventually for Fred and Mary the light of hope replaced the darkness of despair. The Holy Spirit began to reveal to them the deeper meaning of His presence. When this experience becomes real to us, there is for the Christian no hopeless situation.

It is the reality of God, and the sense of His presence in our lives that make the final difference between despair and hope.

Fred and Mary regained confidence and strength for victorious living when they discovered that Christ has conquered even death. In their time of need, they discovered a deeper ministry of the Holy Spirit than they had known before. They began to understand from experience what before they had known only intellectually: "We know that in all things God works for the good of those who love him" (Rom. 8:28, NIV).

In announcing His mission in the world, Jesus quoted from Isaiah: "The Spirit of the Sovereign Lord is upon me, because the Lord has anointed me . . . to comfort all who mourn . . . to bestow on them a crown of beauty instead of ashes, the oil of gladness instead of mourning, and a garment of praise instead of a spirit of despair" (Isa. 61:1-3, NIV).

HOPE AS CHRISTIAN EXPECTATION

The New Testament is laced with references to hope. Even a modest concordance lists nearly a full column of passages. "The creation waits in eager expectation" (Rom. 8:19, NIV). "In this hope we were saved" (v. 24, NIV). There is "hope . . . stored up for you in heaven" (Col. 1:5, NIV). "Christ in you [is] the hope of glory" (v. 27, NIV). The "resurrection of Jesus Christ from the dead," says Peter, "has given us new birth into a living hope" (1 Pet. 1:3, NIV). One cannot understand the New Testament faith without some comprehension of the term *hope.*

Hope Brings Assurance

Current Christianity has well-nigh lost the biblical meaning of hope. In some instances it has been understood to be a rather anemic or foggy wish. But it is more than that. Hope brings confidence and strength.

Most of us have heard preachers who put a strong emphasis upon what they call "know-so salvation." They would assure their hearers that God had an experience for Christians that would bring such certainty to their hearts that they would truly know that they were saved. They contrast this "know-so salvation" with a "hope-so" brand of religion. Such preachers rightly highlight an important element of the New Testament gospel. The hymn writer called it "blessed assurance." But the association of "hope" with "think" and "maybe" does a grave disservice to the abiding quality of hope.

Hope that brings assurance is essential to survival. The Freds and Marys of the world have sought comfort from their pastors and all too often have been given merely intellectual explanations of the creeds. There has been little of the vitality and verve that is the essence of Christian hope. No wonder so many collapse in the midst of their gloom.

The biblical meaning of hope must be retrieved and applied in the context of 20th-century realities. This hurting world cries out for a message of assurance.

Hope Is Basic

Hope cannot be associated with "think" and "maybe." To do so would be to destroy its abiding quality. At the same time, hope must not be confused with faith, or at least not be considered synonymous with it. The 13th chapter of First Corinthians makes it clear that there are three distinct spiritual foundations which abide (endure)—faith, hope, and love. Faith and hope are not the same but they are mutually supportive. Hope is dynamic—it draws us on.

It is hard to understand why we have allowed hope to become merely a secondary shadow of faith. In doing so we have ended up with only two abiding qualities—faith and love. Clearly, faith and hope, while interrelated, are distinct from each other. Each is necessary to the believer.

It was in the 1960s that the Christian world began talking again about hope and its significance. Jurgen Moltmann, one of the key spokesmen of this movement, distinguished between faith and hope as follows: "Faith is the foundation upon which hope rests; hope nourishes and sustains faith. Without faith's knowledge of Christ, hope becomes a utopia and remains hanging in the air. But without hope, faith falls to pieces, becomes a fainthearted and ultimately dead faith."[1]

There can be no hope without faith. But hope is much more than a vain wish. It is more than a secondary shadow of faith.

Without hope, faith is lifeless. Faith believes that Christ is Lord. Hope eagerly expects that He will demonstrate that Lordship.

Hope Anticipates

"Hope that is seen is no hope at all. Who hopes for what he already has? But if we hope for what we do not yet have, we wait for it patiently" (Rom. 8:24-25, NIV). There is a dynamic not-yet-ness about hope. It is "not yet" because it is unrealized. It is dynamic because it is alive with the expectation that God will do what He has promised.

Hope enables faith to lean expectantly toward its own future. Hope acknowledges that "here we do not have an enduring city" (Heb. 13:14, NIV) and constantly probes faith, stimulating it against its inclination to settle down into wooden creeds. Hope anticipates that the God who always goes before us is working redemptively so that no day, however dark, is shut off from God's glorious tomorrow.

Hope's Foundation

The future toward which hope leans is assured by the redemptive activity of the faithful God. This God of hope is more than a God of contemplation. He is God in the midst of history. He is the God of promise who is known by seeing and hearing, by identification and obedience. He is the God of Abraham, Isaac, and Jacob, who weaves His own future into the future of an unworthy people by way of promise and covenant.

1. The God of hope demonstrated His redemptively creative activity in the creation of the universe. From the formless void He created a universe that He could call "very good" (Gen. 1:31).

2. Throughout ancient Hebrew history God proved himself again and again as a redemptive agent who brought help and hope to His people. He caused a bush to flame, He sent plagues, He held back a sea, He caused water to spring forth from a rock, He sent food from heaven, He stopped a river, He directed a stone from a shepherd's sling, He caused the sun to stand still.

3. But the event above all others that displays the faithfulness of God and the greatness of His power is the resurrection of Jesus. Even though Jesus submitted himself to death—the ultimate hopelessness—the God of hope proved himself to be faithful through the event of the Resurrection. The Resurrection is the fulfillment of all past promises.

It is a historic event, not just because it happened in history, but because it breaks new ground for the future. It *makes* history just as the first creation did. Through it, promise and fulfillment find new form. They are bound up in Jesus Christ through whom God has laid the groundwork for the future of mankind. Latent in the resurrection of Jesus is the promise of God to bring salvation to us individually and to His total creation.

The crucifixion and the resurrection of Jesus rest on the faithfulness of God and are the foundation of realistic hope. As Peter testifies, the resurrection of Jesus Christ from the dead "has given us new birth into a living hope" (1 Pet. 1:3, NIV).

Hope's Future Focus

While hope grows out of these historic events, hope itself does not look backward but forward. As Christians we look back and acknowledge that God acted in creation and all natural life is a confirming testimony to that creation. We look back to declare the resurrection of Jesus as the means by which we become new creatures. But we also hear the voice of Jesus speaking through the Revelator declaring, "I am making everything new!" (Rev. 21:5, NIV).

Out of nothing the Eternal Word spoke a universe into existence. Out of the hopelessness of the tomb He broke forth to life eternal. He is our Creator. He is our Redeemer.

But He is also our coming King. Hope still leans forward to anticipate that "him who is, and who was" is also Him, "who is to come" (Rev. 1:4, NIV). Jesus Christ, who is never limited by the apparent "potential" of the situation, always works creatively to bring the "truly new" to pass. He is the object of our hope from first to last. It has been well said, "Jesus is not only the Alpha point—the beginning point—but He is also the Omega point—the ending point—standing beyond time and at the end of history, drawing all things toward himself."

THE SECOND COMING OF CHRIST

There are aspects of the Second Coming that are hard to understand. The details of time and sequence are debated by earnestly sincere people. This confusion springs from the fact that we are a part of the old order. What Jesus will do in His second coming is as uniquely new as the Genesis creation, or the Resurrection. The old simply cannot fully comprehend it. The best we may expect is to "see but a poor reflection" (1 Cor. 13:12, NIV).

But this we confidently declare. The God who goes before us has never been limited by the circumstances. He is not an inventor who devises machines from existing materials. He is a Creator. He makes things new. He has worked after that fashion in the past. He will work after that fashion in the future. His second coming is the ultimate declaration that there are no hopeless situations! He will make all things new and they will be right.

This belief in the second coming of Christ is a key doctrine of the Church. It is full of assurance which is the substance of hope.

The Resurrection

The individual who is spiritually prepared is assured of heaven after death. Our 16th Article of Faith declares,

> We believe in the resurrection of the dead, that the bodies both of the just and of the unjust shall be raised to life . . . We believe that glorious and everlasting life is assured to all who savingly believe in, and obediently follow, Jesus Christ our Lord.

This truth enables a believer to be filled with hope and so to confidently approach the moment of his death in anticipation of his glorification.

The Risen Saints

The Church struggles through an unbelievable variety of distresses in the hope of the Second Coming, at which time the

Church Militant will become the Church Triumphant. Our Articles of Faith further declare:

> We believe that the Lord Jesus Christ will come again; that we who are alive at His coming shall . . . be caught up with the risen saints to meet the Lord in the air, so that we shall ever be with the Lord (Article XV, par. 19).

Redemption for the World

The whole universe awaits its redemption. All that exists was created by the Living Word and it was declared "very good" (John 1:3). Then sin defiled the order of the cosmic world. The resulting natural evil brought its disorder. Pain became a part of life. "The whole creation has been groaning in travail" (Rom. 8:22, RSV). But in hope we declare that "the creation itself will be liberated from its bondage to decay and brought into the glorious freedom of the children of God" (Rom. 8:21, NIV). There will be a "new heaven and a new earth" (Rev. 21:1).

All of this declares that for the believer, for the Church, and for the universe itself, there is no hopeless situation. The God who has acted, is now acting—and will act again.

THE FINAL HOPELESSNESS

The hope of mankind rests in God and in what He has done for us in Christ. The *Manual* affirms what the Bible teaches that

> the atonement through Jesus Christ is for the whole human race; and that whosoever repents and believes on the Lord Jesus Christ is justified and regenerated and saved from the dominion of sin (par. 26.5).

But the Bible also teaches the hopeless outlook for those who are without God. Paul reminds early Christians of their hopeless condition before they found new life in Christ. "At that time you were separate from Christ . . . without hope and without God in the world" (Eph. 2:12, NIV).

Unless men find new life in Christ they remain without God, and without hope—both in this life and in the next.

The Resurrection of Damnation

We have already noted our belief "in the resurrection of the dead, that the bodies both of the just and the unjust shall be raised to life." For those who have done good, this will be "the resurrection of life." But for those who have done evil, it becomes "the resurrection of damnation."

The Judgment

The Bible teaches, "It is appointed unto men once to die, but after this the judgment" (Heb. 9:27). We do not know a great deal about the details of the final judgment, but on the basis of biblical teaching the church asserts: "We believe in future judgment in which every man shall appear before God to be judged according to his deeds in this life" (*Manual*, Article XVI, par. 21).

Final Destiny

"We believe that glorious and everlasting life is assured to all who savingly believe in, and obediently follow, Jesus Christ our Lord" (par. 22). This is the Christian hope.

But there is the dark underside of this truth. The Bible teaches, "If we deliberately keep on sinning after we have received the knowledge of the truth, no sacrifice for sin is left, but only a fearful expectation of judgment and of raging fire that will consume the enemies of God" (Heb. 10:26-27, NIV).

The Bible teaches, and we believe "that the finally impenitent shall suffer eternally in hell" (Article XVI, par. 22). To be forever separated from God is to lose all hope. It is the ultimate hopelessness.

HOPE AS CHRISTIAN VITALITY

But while there is life, there is hope. Where there is new life in Christ, there is Christian hope. Such hope reflects on the past, leans toward the future, and brings strength to the present. It has a here-and-now quality. It produces an energy for survival that is otherwise missing.

Ancient Israel Hoped in God's Promise

The covenant people were able to endure unspeakable hardship and survive generations of captivity because deep within them they knew that the God of creation, the God of Abraham, Isaac, and Jacob, was at work. In time He would do "His mighty redemptive acts" on behalf of His people. This hope enabled them to survive what other peoples, less persecuted, were unable to bear.

The Early Christians Found Hope in the Cross

Jesus was obedient even to death on a cross. That cross, a symbol of man's hate, became the symbol of God's love. He took the angry instrument of His own Son's execution and made of it the vehicle for the salvation of the world. Here is creative power no less potent than that described in Genesis. And the disciples learned that the "God of hope" could do that to their personal crosses as well. They faced the ugly cross with eyes wide open and saw the glory of the resurrection in it. They endured persecution beyond imagination with the "patience of hope" (1 Thess. 1:3). Hope was their "helmet" of defense (1 Thess. 5:8). Death was no threat to them because their hope was founded beyond this life (1 Cor. 15:19).

We Can Know the Vitality of Hope

I would not mislead you. I wish I could tell you that as far as Fred and Mary are concerned, all is well. At this writing I cannot. The prognosis is still very serious. But Mom and Dad have found the presence of Jesus Christ as Creator, Redeemer, and Coming King. They believe that His creative power can bring complete healing, and they continue to pray that He will do so.

They are confident that what the *Manual* says is right: "We believe the Bible doctrine of divine healing and urge our people to seek to offer the prayer of faith for the healing of the sick" (Article XIV, par. 18). They and others who have supported them during these dark days have sincerely prayed this prayer. But they have also followed through on the second part of the paragraph,

"Providential means and agencies when deemed necessary should not be refused" (par. 18). The situation is completely in God's hands.

Best of all, they rejoice in the evidence of Christ's redemptive power that has not only saved them but constantly comforts them. They realize also that the Master's creative touch may come to Danny through death and Danny would enter the "new kingdom" ahead of them. None of these options are hopeless. All are within the domain of the wise and able Jesus.

This does not mean that they do not hurt. There is glory in their cross, but it is still a cross. And any cross is characterized by some sense of loneliness and the question, "Why?" But it is never, ever hopeless.

At age 87, the well-known evangelist and author, E. Stanley Jones, suffered a paralyzing stroke. Through much difficulty he dictated his last book titled, *The Divine Yes*. He cited 2 Cor. 1:19-20 (Moffatt) as his text. "The divine 'yes' has at last sounded in him, for in him is the 'yes'" to all of life's noes. Holding up the resurrection of Jesus as the ultimate, divine affirmation, he asked, "How far can evil go in a world of this kind? Does the moral universe bend to evil? The answer is NO! Today, tomorrow, but the third day—NO! The third day, evil breaks itself upon the facts of life."[2]

To all of us who, like Fred and Mary, are going through the black Friday or dark Saturday of our lives, I speak with great respect and understanding. The cross is ugly and hurts desperately. The circumstances do appear hopeless. But our God is not the God of the circumstances. He is the Creator God who brings the truly new. Joy comes in the morning.

> *My hope is built on nothing less*
> *Than Jesus' blood and righteousness. . . .*
> *When all around my soul gives way,*
> *He then is all my Hope and Stay.*
> *On Christ, the solid Rock, I stand;*
> *All other ground is sinking sand.*
>
> —EDWARD MOTE

Notes

CHAPTER 3

1. W. T. Purkiser, *Adventures in Truth* (Kansas City: Beacon Hill Press of Kansas City, 1969), 9.
2. Ralph Earle, *How We Got Our Bible* (Kansas City: Beacon Hill Press of Kansas City, 1971), 119.
3. William Barclay, *Fishers of Men* (Philadelphia: Westminster Press, 1966), 26.

CHAPTER 7

1. Adapted from *With Christ in the School of Prayer,* by Andrew Murray (Old Tappan, N.J.: Fleming H. Revell Co., 1953, reprint).

CHAPTER 8

1. Charles L. Allen, *What I Have Lived By* (Old Tappan, N.J.: Fleming H. Revell Co., 1976), 22.

CHAPTER 9

1. Dietrich Bonhoeffer, *Letters and Papers from Prison* (New York: Macmillan Co., 1967).
2. Lyle Jacobson, *Home and Church: Ministering to Youth* (Glendale, Calif.: Regal, 1977).

CHAPTER 10

1. Jurgen Moltmann, *The Theology of Hope,* trans. James W. Leitch (New York: Harper and Row, 1967), 44.
2. E. Stanley Jones, *The Divine Yes* (Nashville and New York: Abingdon Press, 1975), 106.

Appendix

Suggested books for additional reading:

Power Through Prayer, E. M. Bounds
The Spirit of Holiness, Everett Cattell
Holiness and Human Nature, Leon and Mildred Chambers
My Utmost for His Highest, Oswald Chambers
Streams in the Desert, Mrs. Charles E. Cowman
Keep the River Flowing, Sylvia Culver
The Fullness of the Spirit, William Greathouse
Holiness and High Country, A. F. Harper
The Kneeling Christian, By an Unknown Christian
The Cycle of Victorious Living, Earl Lee
Mere Christianity, C. S. Lewis
With Christ in the School of Prayer, Andrew Murray
The Autobiography of God, Lloyd Ogilvie
The Power of Your Attitudes, Leslie Parrott
What Is Sanctification? Leslie Parrott
The Christian's Secret of a Happy Life, Hannah Whitall Smith
The Disciplined Life, Richard S. Taylor
Life in the Spirit, Richard S. Taylor
The Best of A. W. Tozer, Compiled by Warren Wiersbe